PING-PONG
IS NOT A
STRATEGY

*How to Create an Awesome
Organization Culture*

BY

MATT R. VAADI

CONTENTS

CHAPTER 4: FINDING THE RIGHT PEOPLE FOR YOUR CULTURE . . .49

CHAPTER 5: SCREENING AND SELECTION. 63

ACKNOWLEDGEMENTS

I originally took on this project thinking it would be easy. I would string together some of my old writings into a short book that could be used as a marketing piece. A year later, I am finally writing this acknowledgement and preparing for it to go to press. Needless to say, there are a lot of people that have helped me along the way.

First, I would like to thank my amazing wife. You are my everything. I love you more than words could ever express. Thank you for always being by my side. Thank you to Elle and Colt for always making me smile. You bring great joy to my life. I love you both dearly.

I would like to thank my church family. While I never asked for prayers about this project, I know you were praying for my success and I felt it.

Thank you to my family—the Vaadis, Parodys, Caulders, Komorniks, and Koehlers. You are all amazing and give me strength every day to try to get better. A special shout-out to my sister, Ginger. You have always been there for me, even from afar.

For those of you that helped me write this book, I am forever in your debt. Alicia MacDonald and Ginny Glass are master editors. Thank you for all of your help and suggestions to take the ramblings of my mind to the public.

I would also like to thank all of the people who shared information about their companies to give me the great insights included in this book. I did not create these best practices, I just stole them from the best. A special thanks to Shawn Regan, Matt Telmanik, and Tom Pietras for spending the additional time with me.

To my mother, I miss you every day. I know you would be proud to see this book published since all of my creativity comes from you.

Thank you to our Lord and savior, Jesus Christ, for dying on the cross for our sins.

INTRODUCTION

HOW DO YOU KNOW IF THIS BOOK IS FOR YOU?

Before getting started, ask yourself these questions:

1. Do you believe your employees are your company's most important asset?
2. Are you committed to building the type of place people want to work?
3. Are you willing to step outside your comfort zone to make that happen?

If you answered yes, keep reading. If you answered no to any of these, but are open to being convinced, keep reading. If you are close-minded, go ahead and grab another book off the shelf.

WHAT CAN THIS BOOK DO FOR YOU?

Ping-Pong Is Not A Strategy is a collection of my anecdotes, experiences, and interviews conducted over the years as an HR professional. This book provides you with the framework needed to spark a positive change in your workplace, not just for yourself and your team—but for the future of your organization.

WHY IS THIS BOOK IMPORTANT?

If you want to create a great workplace culture, use this book as your map for how to get there. This strategy is not about creating something entirely new or flashy—or even being the best in your industry. The book is designed to help you understand how you can create the type of work environment that excites your team. It sounds like a simple plan, as most do until it is time to execute it.

HOW TO USE THIS BOOK

This book does not need to be read sequentially, nor do you need to implement every strategy I recommend to see change within your workplace. The most important step when deciding to use this book is getting started. If there is a chapter that sparks your initial interest more than another, that's great—start there. Over time, you may find that another chapter represents a newly developed weakness that your workplace can improve upon.

This book should be scribbled in, skipped around, and referenced. I have included templates, worksheets, and references to online resources throughout the chapters. You will find what you need to improve your company's culture within the pages of this book. There are no secrets to a great culture. You just need to be intentional and consistent—with the will to get things started.

MY STORY

The sound of the siren woke me up. We lived right across the street from the local fire department in a small, sleepy town in upstate NY. They had an old siren on a street pole that would wail every time there was a fire to crack the volunteer firefighters into action. I fell back asleep, thinking nothing of it. This was a regular occurrence. Our small apartment was above a local bar, across the street from a fire station. Being awakened in the middle of the night was a regular occurrence. But something was different about this night—to put it lightly, it changed the course of my life forever.

When I woke the next morning, the answering machine (*this was the thing we had before voicemail on cell phones for you young folks out there*) was flashing red; several voicemails had come through while I laid asleep...

My mother had been badly hurt. She was attacked by a disgruntled customer while at work. She would die hours later in the hospital from wounds. She was tending bar, alone, on a Friday night/Saturday morning on a backroad in upstate NY. She was 36 years old. I miss her every day.

That day changed my life in so many ways it is hard to count. She was single with my dad out of the picture. I was 14 years old and I moved in with my aunt and uncle (who I am forever grateful for). They did everything they could to keep me on the straight and narrow (which did not work very well in my youth, but they certainly tried). In recent years, as I approached the age my mother passed away, life's uncertainty has become more and more impactful to my perspective on work and workplaces.

I have been working since I was 15 years old—from the fast-food line at Taco Bell, to making hundreds of thousands of dollars in software sales leadership. Throughout my experiences, I have seen great workplace cultures firsthand. But, amid the great lies the terrible—those workplaces that I could never really shake from memory.

However, the one thing that has remained constant during my career is the role that my workplace and work-family play in my life. Culture and environment within any workplace have a cascading effect. That is why it is so important for me to help employers and small business owners create a better place for their teams to work.

Doing work that does not matter is not an option anymore. Life is too short to continue doing work that is not fulfilling—it's time to start positively serving others. It sounds easier said than done, I understand that. But the good news is we all have choices, including you and every member of your team. If you cannot create the type of work environment that gets your team excited to come to work every day, then they can, and will, go somewhere else. Say yes to today and begin on the path toward creating a great workplace culture.

BAD JOBS

Have you ever had a job you did not like? I have. <u>It sucks.</u>

 Who else does it impact when you do not like your job?

It made my spouse crazy because she just wanted me to be happy, my friends were tired of listening to me bitch, and I was miserable to people I worked with. It was not a good time. Every day I felt like my work did not matter and I just wanted to get the day over. What a waste.

What do you think would happen if you made one of your teammates happier to come to work every day? *How big could the ripple effect get?*

When a happy teammate goes home and treats their spouse better, who treats their children better, who treats other kids better at school, and spreads positivity, how far does it go?

To me, the impact of a great workplace culture knows no bounds. Your impact could change families, the community, and the world. Do not underestimate your ability as a leader to change lives by creating the type of place people want to work.

In 2010, I worked for a large corporation when my wife and I decided we wanted to move to Columbia, SC from Raleigh, NC. We planned on living in SC for a long time since the reason we were moving was to get closer to family and start one of our own. This created a feeling of wanting to "nest" in the community. This meant I was committed to getting more involved than I ever would have in Raleigh, which was more of a transient environment. We wanted to put roots down in the community.

Since early in my career, I realized that getting involved with charitable causes was not only a great way to advance their cause but also network and team build in the process. One of our favorite local charities was having a 5k and this was the perfect opportunity for our team to volunteer and sponsor the event to get our brand associated with something good happening in our new community in SC. I called up to "corporate" one day to ask for a few hundred dollars to sponsor the event and was disappointed with the result.

"Matt, we just don't get involved at the local level."

I remember this conversation clear as day. My family and I were putting down roots in South Carolina and wanted to be a part of the community. For us, this meant supporting causes we cared about and being a part of a company that cared about our community.

When I could not find a company in my industry that aligned with these goals, I created it. That is how ERG Payroll & HR was born.

The entrepreneurial dream was alive.

We chose to give away 5 percent of our company to local charities. That includes 3 percent of all revenue, 1 percent of our services, and 1 percent of our time volunteering (come serve with us!).

This does not mean that you have to go out and start your own small business to create a positive shift in your workplace. The change begins with you. What is it about your company that makes it a unique place to work? How will you create an environment that excites your team? These questions and more will be answered throughout the book, so let us keep moving forward.

INSPIRE THE CULTURE

When I started ERG Payroll & HR, hundreds of companies told me they needed more HR support, but contacting a call center was not appealing. They needed more than just an online system and someone in another zip code whom they had never met. They wanted people who knew their business and cared about them. They wanted someone who cared about their culture as much as they did.

As a company, our Vision is "To be the Most Trusted Provider of HR Solutions."

We are working toward this by trying to make our clients' workplaces better. If you have ever been unhappy at work, you know how many lives that can impact. Your unhappiness can hurt your team, your family, and your own physical and mental health.

Conversely, if we can make one person happier to come to work every day, there is no telling how far that positivity will spread. Will that person treat others better? Will they treat themselves better? Will they be more productive? The data says yes. That is why we love doing what we do. We will look at the data and case studies in the coming chapters.

Over the past 15 years, I have consulted with over 1,000 companies as an HR leader and entrepreneur. I have taken what I learned from those conversations to create the ultimate guide on how to create a fantastic place to work. This book is written for entrepreneurs and company leaders who want to develop a culture that people get excited to work in. Join me as we move toward making a positive impact on your workplace environment.

THE IMPORTANCE OF MINDSET

Creating an awesome culture is not easy. As the title states, it is not as simple as putting a ping pong table in the breakroom. It is a commitment that takes a lot of time and energy. A great culture starts with the right mindset.

A study was carried out in Japan on 13 people who were extremely allergic to poison ivy. Each was rubbed on one arm with a harmless leaf but was told it was poison ivy and touched on the other arm with poison ivy and told it was harmless. *All 13* broke out in a rash where the harmless leaf contacted their skin. Only two reacted to the poison leaves.[1]

This study reminds me of a client meeting I once had. The client had a string of bad hires over a while and began to let negativity overtake his hiring processes.

"We can't get top talent here, we are in this office that we lease, we don't have a white-collar office, and we are a small business. We can't compete with the other companies with bigger budgets."

> *How can you get top talent and create an awesome culture if you don't believe you can?*

You are done before you start. If you want to create a "Best Place to Work," it has to start with the right mindset. The biggest mindset issue we have is that people don't think it matters. They think that by giving someone a job and a paycheck, they should be eternally grateful and thank their lucky stars. No one thrives

---

[1] http://www.nytimes.com/1998/10/13/science/placebos-prove-so-powerful-even-experts-are-surprised-new-studies-explore-brain.html

in that environment. If they stay, they will not give you their best, but they are much more likely to leave and find someone who cares. *A company that cares.* Let's go on the path to be that company together.

In this book, I am going to give you the blueprint to create the best place to work. All you must do is follow it. **Let's go!**

CHAPTER 1:

THE IMPACT
OF A BAD CULTURE

"Nothing in the world is worth having or worth doing unless it means effort, pain, difficulty ... I have never in my life envied a human being who led an easy life. I have envied a great many people who led difficult lives and led them well."
— **Theodore Roosevelt**

Every year, Gallup surveys companies about employee engagement[2]. For the last several years, the number of employees that are actively engaged has hovered around 30 percent. If only 30 percent of your employees are engaged, that means you have more than a few miserable people on your team. The good news is that this number is on the rise.

Do not believe the studies that only 30 percent of people are actively engaged? Close your eyes and picture 10 people from your company around a table at the start of a team meeting.

There will be three people on one end that cannot turn it off. They were early to the meeting. They are "in it to win it." They are always willing to do what it takes to get the job done. At the other end of the table, there will be another few prepared for the meeting. Unfortunately, they are still talking about the game last night. They show up right on time or a little late and they go through the motions. Then there will be a couple who roll their eyes at everything and cannot wait to get out of there. They are checking their phones to see if that recruiter on LinkedIn got back to them.

If you are not seeing this, you are either not paying attention or you are in the minority.

---

2   *https://news.gallup.com/poll/241649/employee-engagement-rise.aspx*

What difference does it make?

We can all picture the above situation. However, there is one fact that tends to get lost with employers.

The 30 percent of employees that are actively engaged *outperform the other 70 percent by over 200 percent*[3].

Stop and read that again. *200 percent.*

That is an astonishing number. The top 30 percent of your team will outproduce the rest by 200 percent. It begs the question; what if we can improve that number to 40 percent? What about 50 percent? How do we get more people into the "actively engaged" category?

Not to mention, when you have to let one of those people from the 70 percent go, it is going to cost you a lot of money to replace them. You are paying a lot of money to replace the least productive people on your team. *That is a tragedy.*

WHAT KIND OF PLACE DO YOU WANT TO WORK IN?

We all have had jobs we did not like, and we know how to avoid creating that type of environment. As a business owner, I am driven to create the type of workplace where my team and I want to work.

But I will be honest with you; having a great workplace culture was not always the reality for me. I have worked in environments where I did not want to come to work. I would dread seeing my boss's name show up on my cell phone. I knew that it was going to be a painful rehashing of a conversation we already had. It was brutal.

When you start your own company, you can craft the culture from the ground up. You have the unique opportunity to create the place you want to work and find others who will enjoy that. It is a little more complex when you're in a place of leadership at a

---

[3] *https://www.dalecarnegie.com/en/resources/emotional-drivers-of-employee-engagement*

company that you didn't start. That is not to say it isn't possible to spark a change, because it very much is. You may just have a few more obstacles and hoops to jump through.

But where could it all go wrong?

Well, it all starts with the mindset of the business owner, and trickles down to the leadership team and beyond.

If a business owner is stuck in a negative mindset, which then impacts how invested the leadership team is to create a great culture, will a good hire be able to overcome it? In truth, the answer is no. You cannot have one person rowing in the opposite direction and still make it to your destination. Let's see what could happen when you make a bad hire on the leadership team.

HOW BIG OF AN IMPACT CAN ONE BAD BOSS MAKE?

At the ERG Payroll & HR Executive Summit in 2016, we had a panel on "How to Create an Awesome Workplace." David Dunn from VC3, a Managed Services Provider in Columbia, SC, shared with the group about how they created their culture.

As a company, they were regularly placed in the top ten on the "Best Places to Work in South Carolina" list presented by SC Biz News and the South Carolina Chamber of Commerce. That year, they dropped from the top of the rankings to last out of the companies selected. They had been on this list for several years and did not expect 2016 to be any different.

When they got the results back and found that they were last on the list, they were surprised. Their team did not expect anything to be different since not much had changed from previous years. While they were still one of the best places to work in South Carolina, they became the worst of the best.

WHAT WAS DIFFERENT THAT YEAR?

The way these "Best Places to Work" lists are created is by surveying employees on a variety of topics. When you reach a certain size (number of employees), you get the data back and it's broken down by department.

When the leadership team at VC3 started reviewing the data, they realized that all the bad surveys stemmed from one department, with one less than stellar manager.

One bad boss was able to take them from a top ten spot on "Best Place to Work" to the worst on the list.

The proverbial "one bad apple ruins the bunch" applies to culture more than anywhere else.

If all this is so obvious and the numbers rarely change, it begs the question; *why are there so many toxic workplaces?*

There are a few reasons.

The first one being that it is easier to maintain the status quo rather than invoke change.

Whether you are building your culture from the ground up or you are trying to change the long-established dysfunction at your place of employment, this first reason is crucial to understand. In the workplace and life, it is sometimes easier to avoid confrontation or change. We all have probably had experiences with that at one point or another. But what happens when that lack of attention to the underlying issues boils over? A toxic work environment is born.

All the things you will learn in this book are simple, but not easy. It takes a lot of time and energy to create a great place to work. You must be faithful and believe that the "juice is worth the squeeze." You must understand that creating a better culture is going to create more productive people. These people will stay with you longer and are happier in the workplace. That does not show up on a spreadsheet for years sometimes.

A lot of leaders will rely on the "that's the way it has always been done" or "turnover is a fact of life in our industry" mentality. Howard Schultz from Starbucks believed that the service industry could change. Starbuck did not have to be doomed to high turnover and low engagement. If he did not believe, where do you think they would be now?

There is also the idea that culture will form organically. We all come from different work cultures, ones that have been great experiences and others that have not been so favorable. As a leader of your team, you must understand that not every person you hire, no matter how "good," will understand your expectations for a positive work culture right off the bat. You do not need to create it, it will happen. That is true, but it will rarely end up the way you hope.

You need to lay the groundwork. If you are reliant on other people to take the reins of your workplace culture, it could end up going in a direction that you had not anticipated. You have no control over the final product if you do not act. You could create everything you fear by not creating anything at all.

WHAT TO EXPECT FROM THIS BOOK

In this book, I am going to show you how to create a great culture. The information provided is based on the areas that are evaluated when you apply to become a "Best Place to Work." While there is no agreed-upon format for all surveys, there are common themes in each. Below are just some of the areas and questions we will cover throughout this book:

- **Learning, Growth, and Advancement:** How do you provide opportunities for your team to learn and develop. How happy are they with those resources and plans?
- **Feedback and Recognition:** Do your employees feel like they are recognized for what they do? How can you make it part of the fabric of your culture to recognize a job well done?
- **Trust:** How comfortable are your employees with the leadership team and the decisions they make?

- **Innovation:** Are you introducing new methods or ideas that benefit the workplace? Are you staying ahead of the competition?

- **Leadership:** How satisfied is your team with leadership and the role their input plays in making a change?

- **Autonomy/Responsibility:** Do your employees feel that they have a role in making decisions and offering feedback about the organization as a whole?

- **Job Requirements:** Does the employee's job allow them to demonstrate their skill set?

- **Interpersonal Relationships:** How do your employees feel about the people they work with?

- **Outcomes:** How satisfied are your employees with going to work every day? How much would they recommend working for your company?

While I did not take each one of these topics and write a chapter on them, I did provide the tools needed to create the results. For example,, there is no chapter on *Trust,* but I show you how to create, communicate, and live your Core Values, which we will cover in this book as well. The Core Values for your company are the foundation for building trust. Additionally, I teach you how to be consistent and communicate effectively with your team. These actions will lead to the trust you desire.

CHAPTER 1 TAKEAWAYS

So, what were the most important lessons learned in Chapter 1?

- "Actively engaged" employees outperform the rest of the team. We will talk about how to get more of your team engaged in the following chapter.

- The mindset of an entire leadership team can negatively impact how well a "good" hire does their job.

- Although it may be easier to stick to the status quo, when you invoke change in the workplace, you begin toward the path of an awesome culture people want to work in.

- If you don't take action about where your workplace is headed, it will eventually end up way off course.

Let's dive into where culture begins—the environment you create.

CHAPTER 2:

ENVIRONMENT

"Life is like a garden; you reap what you sow."
— ***Paulo Coelho***

I was standing in a small warehouse, maybe 20,000 square feet. Behind me was a wall with a whiteboard painted on to it that separated the warehouse where all the equipment was stored from the offices. There were several small offices where the management team worked during the day, and the guys who worked out in the field would pass through each morning and afternoon as they prepared for the job. The company did residential and commercial plumbing work. Good people that seemed to have built a good company.

As I looked at the 25 or so men in front of me, I tried to keep them engaged. They were mostly field workers and were ready to get their day started so they could beat the South Carolina heat and I was the only thing standing in their way. They were not used to an "outsider" coming in and talking to them about employment issues. Particularly not an outsider wearing a blazer, jeans, and nice(ish) shoes. They did not see me as one of them.

We were rolling out their new employee handbook. We had given everyone a copy and I was hitting the highlights. We asked the owner what they wanted us to hit, and we also chose a few sections to cover in detail based on what we had been told about the company.

I was going through with my normal balance of humor and seriousness to try to keep the meeting light—all while getting the key points across. When I came to the drug-free workplace section, I said, "Your company is a drug-free workplace..." This was covered by laughter from the entire team. I was shocked. Did that just happen? Did an entire room of employees just laugh at the statement that their company was a drug-free workplace?

The owner of the company smirked and then tried to say something to edify the crowd that came across as "don't worry, it's just what's in writing." I did my best to not seem completely appalled. I do not like to say I can see the future, but there are certain things that you just know how they end.

About 12 months later, an employee who had been with the company for a few months called into our office. He was upset. He told one of our HR business partners that the two men he shared a truck with would smoke marijuana between jobs (shocker, I know). We let the owner of the company know about the situation and coached him on how to handle it. The owner ignored most of our advice and the employees were all back in the same truck again—but now these guys knew the reporting employee was a snitch. The accused coworkers started harassing the man who voiced his concern and treating him like crap because they knew he had ratted them out. The man who had come to us for assistance came back to let us know he was going to have to quit soon.

In a shocking turn of events, the owner came to us and said that the reporting employee's performance was not up to par. The owner insisted that he needed to write the reporting employee up. He also told us that he wanted to fire that employee as well. Oh boy. That is a bad idea.

The situation continued to unfold with the twists and turns of Space Mountain until ultimately, they did let that reporting employee go a few months later. They had set a precedent for a culture that allowed people to get high and bully people. Their turnover was over 100 percent. They reaped what they sowed.

WHAT DOES A GREAT ENVIRONMENT LOOK LIKE?

Tom Pietras is a Partner at the accounting firm Bauknight Pietras & Stormer, PA. Tom joined Bauknight Pietras & Stormer, PA, in 1992 as a shareholder. He is the firm's director of Accounting and Auditing and is responsible for ensuring that the firm is fully informed of current developments in accounting standards and compliance with the latest auditing standards.

In 1991, several former "Big Four" CPAs decided to establish their firm in Columbia, SC, focused on providing business, financial, and tax solutions to owner-managed companies and wealthy individuals seeking an experienced, innovative, and independent firm immersed in national, state and local business issues. They took all of the good things they had learned from the "big four" about creating a great place to work and created their own "Best Place to Work" that has been recognized as one of the "Best Places to Work" in South Carolina multiple years and counting.

If you know anything about accounting and tax firms, you know they work very long hours during tax seasons, and it can be incredibly stressful work. Tom told me a story about how one Saturday morning when many of the tax associates had come in to meet the deadline, one of the partners brought his waffle maker with him. He set up shop and made breakfast for all of the employees. The company also pays for a monthly food truck for their employees. These are just a few examples of the small things they do to create a great environment. I will be mentioning Tom and BPS throughout this book.

WHAT MAKES A GREAT ENVIRONMENT?

The thing to remember about a great environment is that it is not the same for everyone—that goes for leaders and employees. There are some common themes among the "Best Places to Work," but no two are the same. You cannot fake culture and you cannot hide in your office and hope that others create it for you. You need to create the type of environment that is symbolic of your Core Values and mission. In the coming pages, I will provide you with a guide on how to create or update your Core Values and make sure that your culture is a true reflection of what your company stands for.

SUCCESS IS SIMPLE

One of the dirty little secrets in business is that there are no secrets. Whenever you see someone and say, "How did they grow that fast" or "How do they keep getting all the best talent," it is never luck. It is almost always one simple thing they do better than you: **They execute on the basics.**

I have had the good fortune of knowing Shawn Regan, CEO of Rhythmlink International, for the last five years. His company has been on the "Best Places to Work" in South Carolina and *Inc.* 5000 lists year in and year out. They have experienced exponential growth that is built on doing the small things well, hiring great people, and implementing great systems.

When I interviewed Shawn for this book, he provided me with several profound ideas, and some that were so obvious I had not seen them. That is the thing about building a business; sometimes we fail to see the obvious, and that will be a stumbling block in our process of creating a great work environment. When asked about how Rhythmlink International has continued a path of growth, Shawn had this to say.

"I think we do a better job than most when it comes to execution. One of our Core Values is accountability, which I think is another way of saying execution. If you are trying to attract, retain, and promote people who will be accountable, you have to get things done."

Shawn made mention several times throughout our conversation how there is a great system for everything (hiring, marketing, accounting, etc.). It is a matter of choosing the one that best suits your organization and executing on it.

"You have to do it all well. You cannot have a weak link. You do not have to be the best in the world, you must be a little more than competent. It is not rocket science, but it is hard to do it all well. It is important to do all of the core things good if not better than all of the businesses around you. When you have a couple that you don't do well it just drains you and sucks the life out of the company."

YOUR ENVIRONMENT'S EFFECT ON CULTURE

"Culture eats strategy for breakfast."
— ***Peter Drucker***

When asked if they were intentional about the development of their culture, all of the executives I interviewed from "Best Places to Work" responded with a resounding "yes." Culture is not something that happens by accident. Culture is not something that can be accomplished with a poster on the wall. You need to live, eat, and breathe your mission. Your leadership team should reflect the culture that you want to see across the board. As I mentioned in previous pages, it all begins with leadership. You must believe in what you're trying to accomplish, or it will be nearly impossible to get anyone on your team to join in.

Before we dive into success as a small business, we have to touch base on how exactly to get there. Let's take a look at the "Best Places to Work" that I've mentioned throughout the book thus far. What is it about their companies that has allowed them to create a culture that people want to be a part of?

- **Flexibility**—This comes in a variety of forms from schedules, working from home, and work assignments.
- **Doing the basics very well**—Matt Telmanik made an excellent point about how his team and culture are not flashy, they just consistently do the basics very well.
- **Have substance**—Shawn Regan mentioned how important it is that there is "substance" to what you do, and your team can see the impact you make.
- **Give your team the tools to be successful**—This applies to both hiring and your employees' abilities to do their jobs in the current work setting.

- **Treat everyone the way that you would like them to treat you**—With respect and kindness.
- **Games and incentives**—We heard about all kinds of games, like team trivia and sales contests. A few organizations offered onsite fitness training. Nearly everyone made note of how important it is to <u>have fun</u>.

THE SECRET TO SUCCESS?

I am going to let you in on a little secret to small business success. You will read dozens of books every year and attend seminars all claiming to have the answers to achieving success as a company. I have great news! There are three secrets to creating an amazing company. They are so obvious and so simple you might wonder why you had not thought of them already. Are you ready?

Drumroll please:

Secret #1: Leadership

Secret #2: Leadership

Secret #3: Leadership

Your culture will only be as good as your leadership. Culture is created and formed by the leadership team. If you do not walk the walk and talk the talk, how can you expect anyone else to do the same? **You cannot delegate culture and you cannot delegate leadership.** This is one of the biggest mistakes I see entrepreneurs make. You can't expect someone else to create the culture you envision in your head.

As business owners or leaders within a company, we are all taught to start delegating as much as possible as early as possible so that we can focus on what is important. Do you know what the most important thing to growing your business will be? The right people on your team. You cannot keep, grow, and engage the right people without the right leadership, and that starts with you.

As mentioned in my interview with Shawn, execution is the thing that successful small businesses do better than everyone else. I am going to give you the framework for creating a great culture in the coming pages. All you will need to do is execute.

The following pages include simple systems and processes you can implement at your company to create an awesome culture. Many of these tasks can be delegated once the process is established (things like performance management systems, recognition programs, and employee onboarding), but if your team does not represent your Core Values every day, then they will no longer be at your company's core.

Okay, now take a long look in the mirror and ask yourself are you willing to do the work necessary to create a great place to work? If so, let's keep going.

CHAPTER 2 TAKEAWAYS

Let's reflect on some of the important lessons we learned in Chapter 2.

- You reap what you sow. The consequences of your actions may not be immediate, but they will come.

- Great work environments are never the same. You have to understand your Core Values, which are a reflection of your company as a whole.

- Leadership is the secret to success. Your company's culture is only as good as your leadership.

- You cannot rely on someone else to create the culture you envision. It begins with you.

CHAPTER 3:

CORE VALUES DEFINE YOUR CULTURE

"When you have no target, you will hit it every time."
— **Zig Ziglar**

WHY ARE CORE VALUES IMPORTANT?

There are two ways for culture to be created. You can take the reins as a leader, drive the culture where you want it to go, and create all your processes to coincide with that philosophy, or you can let your team decide what your culture is and become susceptible to the decisions of the mob. *What do you think top-performing organizations do?* The leadership team drives the culture through their actions, storytelling, diligent hiring, and persistence.

Your core values answer several questions for your team and your clients. Why do you exist? What problems are you solving? Why should I work here? Why should I buy from you?

At my company, we create employee handbooks for our clients. The employee handbook is a valuable tool to communicate information to your new hires. This is more than just telling them your inclement weather policy, it is also an opportunity to sit down and review your culture, mission, Core Values, and vision. The document provides a nice outline to discuss both your policies and your expectations and culture.

This reminds me of a client that we made an employee handbook for. When they filled out our questionnaire, they said to just copy and paste the Core Values from another company. Not only did they recommend this, but they also said *any company*, not a specific company. They were willing to take anyone's Core Values and put them in front of a new hire as if they were their own. I was stunned.

Needless to say, their turnover was through the roof. The company was growing and the owners had a vision, but the employees had no idea what that was. They were so protective of information related to growth (upcoming hires, growth metrics, etc.) because they thought any time, they told the employees they were growing, employees would ask for a raise.

While they should have been concerned (they underpaid their people and battled constant turnover as a result), this is not typically the case. While no employee gets excited when you drive up in your new Porsche when they have not had a raise in 10 years, there are ways to communicate a vision, mission, and Core Values that get people excited to be a part of the team.

LAYING THE FOUNDATION

While 36 percent of companies recognize that employee engagement is a top challenge for their company[4], people often forget your Core Values are at the center of driving engagement. They are the blueprint. As I mentioned in Chapter 2, culture is not something that you can accomplish with a poster on the wall. If you cannot explain your blueprint in detail to your leadership team and employees, you won't be able to begin construction on your culture.

We discussed the damage a bad culture can have turnover, lack of engagement, lack of productivity, hoarding of information, and more. Your Core Values are the GPS to make sure those things don't happen. When people don't know your guiding principles and what the company stands for, they assume the worst. People, by nature, with a lack of information, may think that the other party is trying to do them wrong. When you share your Core Values regularly, you give people something to guide their actions and rally around.

---

[4]   https://resources.globoforce.com/research-reports/findings-from-the-shrm-globoforce-employee-recognition-survey-employee-experience-as-a-business-driver

> *"You can't connect the dots looking forward; you can only connect them looking backward."*
> — **Steve Jobs**

CREATING YOUR CORE VALUES

If you already have Core Values, you can still read this chapter to make sure you are getting the most out of those values and that they are appropriate for your company. If you do not have Core Values, this chapter will be an interactive guide to creating and understanding how they align with the type of culture your people can get excited about.

This is not a collection of exercises that should be done by just you or your leadership team. Get your team involved in the efforts so they, too, can feel that they are a part of this change.

However, the Core Values you believe to be true or want to be true might not be a reality. If people are not living the Core Values you set out for the company, you have two options: course correct or adjust. When things are missing from your company culture, that is often a sign that you should act. It is possible to implement a Value that is not currently being done by your company. As I've mentioned in previous chapters, it's all about execution and how you lead your team toward making those Values reflective of your company's core.

This exercise cannot be skipped. Your Core Values will guide your processes for everything—from interviewing and performance management, all the way through to employment separation. You have to know what you stand for so you can make the right decisions.

CORE VALUES EXERCISE

You can find a copy of this exercise at *ergpayroll.com/book*

Provide each of your teammates (or leadership team) with a copy to complete. You will compare the answers afterward. This exercise should only take 15 to 20 minutes for everyone to complete and then allow 30 to 45 minutes for the entire team to review everyone's answers.

You want to keep this to groups of ten people or less. Perform the exercise in workgroups and review with your leadership team depending on the size of your company.

What are the companies that you want to emulate? What do you believe are their Core Values?

_____

Who is the best leader you have ever worked with?

_____

_____

What are the characteristics that define him/ her?

_____

_____

Which positive trait do I see my teammates get complimented on most frequently?

_____

_____

When we are hiring, what is one trait we look for more than any other?

_____

If I could personally have more of one quality instantly, what would it be?

_____

What are the three traits I want my team to recognize me for?

_____

_____

If I were to teach a group of students the most important Values in life for success, what would those be and why?

_____

_____

_____

What Values were important 100 years ago and will be important 100 years from now?

_____

_____

What are the top dozen qualities of the ideal teammate?

_____

_____

_____

_____

Review your answers above. What are the common threads? What things do you consistently recognize as important in yourself and others? List the top fifteen traits below. If you could only recognize these fifteen things, what would they be? *(Use the list of Core Values below to help.)*

1. _____
2. _____
3. _____
4. _____
5. _____
6. _____
7. _____
8. _____
9. _____
10. _____
11. _____
12. _____
13. _____
14. _____
15. _____

Now group any similar Core Values. For example, if you chose both abundance and growth *or* acceptance and compassion, those would be grouped. Use the boxes below to group the Values together.

Choose the one Core Value from each of the five lists above that best represents the label for the entire group. There are no right or wrong answers. These are the basis for creating your Core Values.

_____

_____

_____

_____

_____

List of Core Values

(These are suggestions and there could be more that your team comes up with)

Abundance	Balance	Community
Acceptance	Being the Best	Commitment
Accountability	Benevolence	Compassion
Achievement	Boldness	Cooperation
Advancement	Brilliance	Collaboration
Adventure	Calmness	Consistency
Advocacy	Caring	Contribution
Ambition	Challenge	Creativity
Appreciation	Charity	Credibility
Attractiveness	Cheerfulness	Curiosity
Autonomy	Cleverness	Daring

Decisiveness	Joy	Proactivity
Dedication	Kindness	Professionalism
Dependability	Knowledge	Punctuality
Diversity	Leadership	Recognition
Empathy	Learning	Relationships
Encouragement	Love	Reliability
Enthusiasm	Loyalty	Resilience
Ethics	Making a Difference	Resourcefulness
Excellence	Mindfulness	Responsibility
Expressiveness	Motivation	Responsiveness
Fairness	Optimism	Security
Family	Open-Mindedness	Self-Control
Friendships	Originality	Selflessness
Flexibility	Passion	Simplicity
Freedom	Performance	Stability
Fun	Personal Development	Success
Generosity	Proactive	Teamwork
Grace	Professionalism	Thankfulness
Growth	Quality	Thoughtfulness
Flexibility	Recognition	Traditionalism
Happiness	Risk Taking	Trustworthiness
Health	Safety	Understanding
Honesty	Security	Uniqueness
Humility	Service	Usefulness
Humor	Spirituality	Versatility
Inclusiveness	Stability	Vision
Independence	Peace	Warmth
Individuality	Perfection	Wealth
Innovation	Playfulness	Well-Being
Inspiration	Popularity	Wisdom
Intelligence	Power	Zeal
Intuition	Preparedness	

Compile the answers from each participant onto one sheet and build your list of Core Values. This best occurs as a team meeting where you can whiteboard the most common answers. Now you need to turn them into your language and deliver them in a way that your team can understand.

Before we dive into some real-life examples, I wanted to take a moment to talk about the difference between your Core Values and your mission. The two are similar, but they are not the same. Your Core Values are the who, what, where, when, why of your company—they outline the big ideas that make your company one of a kind. Your mission is a boiled-down version of your Core Values, written in a way that is simple and quick to read.

See the Core Values for ERG Payroll & HR below as an example.

ERG PAYROLL & HR CORE VALUES

Servant Leadership

Serve your team, clients, and community to the best of your ability. The order of this is important. The team first, then clients, then the community. If we serve each other to the best of our ability, we will achieve great things. Teamwork makes the dream work.

Work Hard ... On the Right Things

Prioritize and focus. Show up ready to accomplish the most important tasks first (ABC Priorities, swallow the frog). Be focused on What's Important Now. (W.I.N.)

Fanatical Attention to Detail

Don't take shortcuts. Spend the time to make sure you Only Handle It Once. (O.H.I.O.)

Grow or Die

Have a "+1" Mentality. Be focused on providing service that is one step further than what someone expects. Grow yourself every week both personally and professionally. Be the perfect teammate.

Be Flexible

Life is 10 percent what happens and 90 percent how we react. Remain positive in the face of adversity. Stay calm in the pocket.

Still confused? Check out another example from one of our clients, Pendleton Street Business Advisors.

Pendleton Street Business Advisors helps business owners successfully navigate the most important decisions of their careers. The firm provides financial advice to help founders manage their largest investment: their business.

PENDLETON STREET BUSINESS ADVISORS CORE VALUES

OUR VALUES

Protected Relationships Our clients are the lifeblood of our business. They are why we do what we do. The word client derives from a Latin word whose connotation was "to be under the protection of another." We take the protective aspect of the client very seriously. We also strive to treat one another in our firm as clients of each other. We look after each other's best interests, to the extent we are able. If we do this for ourselves, it will show towards our clients. You can't give what you don't have.

Advice Over Opinions Advice is based on facts, experiences, and expertise. Opinions are mainly based on feelings and subject to influence from the slightest of nudges. Advice stands the test of time and temperament. Opinions are interesting, but probably not worth paying for—and who knows when they'll change?

Revenue Fidelity We consciously and deliberately say no to revenue sources that are not directly paid by our clients to us. In short, our clients are the only people who pay us. We do not accept commissions, kickbacks, finder's fees, or other forms of compensation tied to work we do for and on behalf of our clients.

Ruthless Simplicity Simple is often confused with easy. We think simplicity is the distillation of concepts, facts, and experience into something that can be understood rapidly and put into action by our clients to create peace of mind to realize prosperity. This simplicity could lead to tough changes or hard realizations, but in the end, we think it brings about what our clients want.

Kind Diligence We think of this as a steady pursuit with empathy. We don't want to annoy or pester our clients and colleagues in our quest to respond to their needs, and make sure we get them the information or deliverables they're counting on. We want to take their needs and preferences into account as we deliver our services to them.

Practical Curiosity We seek to blaze paths in our research and analysis for clients, yet not pursue every "rabbit trail" that beckons. This also applies to opportunities we may pursue as a firm. Almost every distraction in life and business comes cleverly disguised as an "opportunity." We seek clarity from our mission statement to apply as a test to these things. It helps to channel our curiosity into something useful and enlightening for the team and our clients.

Value Connectedness We like putting things together. As kids, it was Legos and puzzles, as professionals, it's people and ideas. Even if we're not "engaged" as a firm, we value the making and maintaining of connections. We seek to do this where we can, as often as we can. Everyone wins.

Outcomes Focused As advisors, we sometimes get asked "what should I do?" We don't bring a set of prepackaged bullet points that were recycled among previous engagements to our clients. We seek to understand what they want to accomplish. We want to know what's important to them. We take this information and use it as the template to inform and direct our advice to the client. They create the mold, and we use our expertise and experience to fill it—to their specifications, not ours.

RECOGNIZING ORE VALUES IN ACTION

We will get more into this in Chapter 8, but it cannot be said enough that you need to recognize positive actions more than negative actions. Many leaders find it easy to help correct behaviors, but it can be more challenging to recognize positive actions and tie them back to your Core Values.

What does this look like in action?

An employee has a support call with a client, and you hear them use a keyphrase, solve the client's issue, and offer further support along with providing additional documentation. This aligns with one of your Core Values of "going the extra mile." You take a moment to tell the employee what a great job they did and then email that example to the team, along with the Core Value, so that they understand why it is so important.

During your weekly meeting, you take the time to recognize people who embodied the Core Values during the last week. For example, Pendleton Street Business Advisors has purchased a toy for each of their Core Values and shares them at team meetings with employees who have embodied those characteristics.

At ERG Payroll & HR, we purchased a Buzz Lightyear toy that is passed from teammate to teammate when someone embodies our Core Values at the highest level. We publicly recognize their commitment to our Core Values and cite specific actions that resulted in them being recognized. Not only is this a great opportunity to recognize a teammate, but it also reminds everyone what our Values are and why they are important.

Whether you have a trophy, belt, toy, or award, ensure it is true to your culture and remains consistent with the recognition. This is something that your team needs to be constantly washed in—not a one-time thing.

THE "WHY" BEHIND YOUR VALUES

Having Core Values is great, but it is meaningless if nobody understands why they are essential to your company. In employee surveys we deliver to our client's employees, communication is one of the biggest weaknesses in most organizations. This does not mean how you communicate (email, chat, phone, etc.) it means what you communicate. Employees want to know why their role is important, when they are doing a good job, and what the future of the organization looks like, so they know where they fit in.

THE BEST WAY TO COMMUNICATE WHY YOUR VALUES ARE IMPORTANT

Think like a point guard, not a shooting guard. In basketball, the point guard's job is to run the offense and pass the ball to his teammates. He puts his teammates in a position to score. It is said that great point guards make everyone around them better. A shooting guard is putting themselves in a position to receive the pass and take a great shot when their number is called.

How you communicate the "why" is best handled by passing the ball to someone else instead of shooting yourself. Put them in a great position to score by giving them recognition in front of the team while also allowing your message to get shared by a respected team member.

When recognizing a teammate publicly, ask the team why they feel what you are recognizing the employee for is important. For example: If someone received a testimonial from a client for the great support they provided. After you recognize the great performance by the individual, ask the following questions:

- Why is it important that we provide great service to our clients?
- How does this align with our Core Values?
- Who helped this teammate so they could provide this great support?

The answers you will get from the team will be far more compelling than anything you could say. The result? You will get your team engaged, thinking, and activated. The answers will mean far more to the rest of the team when they come from their peers. You will get the assist *and* the goal.

CHAPTER 3 TAKEAWAYS

Let's reflect on the key points we touched on during Chapter 3.

- Your Core Values are your company's rudder for staying on course. Complete the Core Values exercise with your team.

- Share your Core Values with your team when completed, and then consistently thereafter.

- Recognize your Core Values. Find ways to share when your team is living the Values. <u>Make sure you are leading by example.</u>

- Be a point guard. Ask the right questions to help your team recognize your Core Values. Get the assist, not the goal.

- Write your Core Values on this page. Come back to this when creating your interviewing, hiring, and performance management processes.

CHAPTER 4:

FINDING THE **RIGHT** PEOPLE FOR YOUR CULTURE

"Great vision without great people is irrelevant."
— Jim Collins

HOW CAN YOU CREATE A PROCESS TO FIND THE RIGHT CANDIDATE FOR EVERY ROLE IN YOUR COMPANY?

"Where have you found all of your best teammates in the past?" I asked the CEO.

"Referrals from friends and family," he said.

"How are you currently searching to fill the opening?"

"We have the job posted on Indeed.com."

"Have you exhausted your network?"

"Well, um ... no."

I had this conversation with a client recently, let's just call him Jim Bob to protect his innocence. He was amazed at how simple it was. The same place where he had found all of his best hires in the past (and 60-70 percent of hires come from in the first place) was largely ignored: his network.

He and his team were wasting time filtering through resumes from blind ads (the applicants were not even reading the posting) and dealing with the interviews that staffing agencies were setting. The agencies had no clue what type of person he was looking for and the inbound resumes were becoming overwhelming.

They could have spent far less time by having a few conversations with influencers in the proper circles if they knew what they were looking for. This also would have shortened the hiring cycle and potentially helped to develop future bench strength. Bench strength is achieved when you have candidates who would make

CHAPTER 4: FINDING THE RIGHT PEOPLE FOR YOUR CULTURE 51

good future hires ready for when someone leaves your team. To develop a bench of candidates, you need to be networking and interviewing even when you are not hiring.

The problem was, he did not know what to tell people he was looking for. Telling someone you are looking for a salesperson is rather general. All sorts of people sell all sorts of things.

This conversation led us down the path of creating an employee persona for the role, and ultimately finding the right person by knowing where to look.

HIRING TOP TALENT

Hiring is the most critical part of creating a culture that will engage and retain talented people. You will have to pick the right people to nurture and grow your culture to find more "A" players. The entire cycle is critical, as Shawn Regan explained in our interview:

"For me, one of the biggest moments in our company was when we learned how to hire. Once you know how to hire people, you can fire people. That was a big step for us. Half the time you are afraid of what you don't know, you are afraid of what you are going to find (when you fire someone) and you are going to get another person like them. You can find people who are right for the culture. This makes it so much easier when we find someone who is underperforming or not a fit for the culture. It ended up being a really powerful piece for us."

Your organization is only going to be as successful as the people you hire. Hiring the right people can't happen without the right systems in place.

 "Even a donkey can act like a thoroughbred for three interviews."

My conversation with Shawn reminded me of a quote I heard a long time ago and I think about all the time; "Even a donkey can act like a thoroughbred for three interviews". I am not sure who to attribute that to but I hope it is as helpful to you as it is to me.

"Hiring someone is like everything else, you need a good system. There are multiple systems out there. Once you tap into that, you have the right people in the right seats, you have better, more competent people, your company performance improves ..."

As I've mentioned a couple of times throughout this book, execution is key. You have to use or create a system and follow it.

THE COST OF A BAD HIRE

We are going to refer to the cost of a bad hire several times in this book. It is largely avoidable. The problem is that most people in their haste to get someone (anyone) in their open seat, do not take the small amount of time it takes to prevent many of the bad hiring decisions we have all been guilty of.

A bad hire does more than just waste your time. They can kill your business. Their negative impact can reach your team, clients, vendors, and the families of all those folks. Do not ignore the potentially unfavorable ripple effect of a bad hire. Not only will they cost you a ton of money in hiring expenses, training, and lost productivity, but they can also destroy your efforts to create the culture you envision.

"Should I fire them?" People ask me all the time after giving me a rundown of a situation with an employee. Without all the context, it is very rare I can adamantly say "yes" after one conversation. I have a policy that no one should ever be surprised they are getting fired. They should either have done something so egregious that they know it is a "fireable" offense, or they should be warned and given opportunities to correct their behavior before termination.

This brings me to a call I received from a client last year. He had a teammate who was undermining him behind his back. The client was working hard to create processes, a vision, Core Values, and all the things that could help him take his growing business to the next level. The teammate was polluting the office with jokes and doing things that were the antithesis of their Core Values, simply because she thought it was funny. It would be one thing if she was just playing around, but she was being malicious.

After he walked me through what she was doing and saying, I told him point-blank: You need to fire her. You cannot have a teammate who is going against the direction in which you are trying to intentionally create a culture. When a bad hire knows they are opposing your leadership *and* doing it publicly, there is no chance for resurrection in my book. If someone is too dense to understand that is a bad idea, no amount of time is going to help correct their performance, especially on a small team.

MY TURN FOR A BAD HIRE

I remember it clear as day. It was the middle of her first day on the job and I thought to myself, I cheated the process and I'm going to pay for it. I hired her without going through all of the steps. We had an opening that needed to be filled and I was in a rush so that I did not have to do the work myself. She was already looking at her phone far too often, exposing a lack of talent that did not come through in the interview, and behaving unprofessionally. The more time we spent together, she was changing my opinion about her ability to do the job negatively. She was also clearly not going to fit into our culture. Our people are hyper-focused, and she seemed to be constantly distracted. This was exactly the type of thing we created the hiring process to prevent. Oof.

As an HR professional, I try my best to follow the processes and procedures that we have created and implemented at our clients' sites. We spend a great deal of time, energy, and resources creating processes and evaluating their effectiveness (both internally and with the clients we consult). In this circumstance, I got emotional and took a quick way out, which meant hiring someone who wasn't an "A" player. This was a role that I had tried to fill several times before, and we could not afford the top-quality person we needed. When we finally had the budget, I immediately recognized after just half a day that I had not spent enough time screening this candidate. I did not follow the process and it was going to cost me.

Thankfully, her behavior didn't change much (as expected). She would call out at least once a week, had a lot of trouble focusing on what was happening inside these walls, consistently tending to things other than work while she was in the office (with no attempt to hide it), and she did not have the skill set that she portrayed in the interview process. She was a donkey poorly disguised as a thoroughbred.

After several weeks of a tense working relationship, she texted me one morning and resigned. It was one of the bigger reliefs I have ever had over a resignation. I cheated the process, lost thousands of dollars in wages, and lost production. It cost me the trust of my team and my clients. Please learn from my mistakes. Follow the steps below and drastically improve your success rate with hires you make at your company. This process, when followed, is proven to increase retention by 25-50 percent.

So, what can we do to avoid these types of bad hires in the future? It's simple, but we need to look to marketers for the answers.

WHAT DOES CONTENT MARKETING HAVE TO DO WITH IT?

According to the Content Marketing Institute, content marketing is defined as follows:

"Content marketing is a marketing technique of creating and distributing valuable, relevant, and consistent content to attract and acquire a clearly defined audience – with the objective of driving profitable customer action."

Most companies are not creating or distributing valuable content to promote their organization as a great place to work. More importantly, most companies are not giving talented people a way to take action. Every marketer talks about how important the "call to action" is on a marketing piece. This is the big button that says "click here" or "sign up now" or it is the "call us now" at the end of a television commercial. As an employer, you need to create ways for people to engage with your brand and see your culture on display. This can be as simple as your social media accounts shining a spotlight on your brand, or as comprehensive as in-person hiring events at your company. One thing you must do is give people a way to apply, even when there is not an opening.

The first thing we can take from content marketers is having a clearly defined audience. If you have a sales branch of your organization, you might already be familiar with buyer personas. We can use a variation of this process to identify our target team members. A buyer persona is a profile of the ideal target that you are trying to sell your product or service. Creating a buyer persona allows you to tailor your message to the audience. This helps sales and marketing teams customize their material so it appeals to the unique needs of their buyers. Your team should create an "employee persona" for the ideal candidates you would like to join your company. This will help you to speak directly to the candidates with targeted messaging that is important to them. You should evaluate your compensation plans and benefit packages to meet their unique needs based on these personas.

To have an effective content marketing program that attracts potential clients and meets them where they require takes a great deal of planning. Let's look at the ways that small businesses can use these techniques to drive actions from top recruits to join their team.

THE VALUE OF PERSONAS

Personas allow you to be very targeted and specific with your search. If you are looking for a software engineer and have been posting your jobs on LinkedIn, you might realize that many software engineers do not spend much time on LinkedIn. That would not be the best place to spend your time and money recruiting. You would want to find where the engineers are looking for jobs. What are the meetups or networks where they are most likely to be open to hearing about a new opportunity?

You wouldn't go fishing in the woods. Go fishing where the fish are.

WHAT IS AN EMPLOYEE PERSONA?

Employee Personas are fictional, generalized representations of your ideal employees by role. In the situation above, we created two personas since there were a few ideas about what type of person would be best to fill the role.

The employee persona is used to help you understand your potential employees better and make it easier for you to tailor your recruiting approach, messaging, and compensation package toward what is important to the candidate.

The strongest personas are based on your best former and current employees, or research that you have conducted. Most roles will have multiple personas or variations. It is important to use this process as a filtering technique, not a tool to discriminate. Creating a persona based on Ralph, who was a white male that has been a successful accountant for 10 years, is a CPA, and likes to spend his time with his family, does not mean the next person has to be a white male, the same age, with the same interests.

You need to find the right people with the right skills and understand that diversity of thought and background is also important to any team. These personas should help you to identify what skill sets are most important to you and where to find them.

Creating an employee persona should be the first step in recruiting. This process follows the same logic as marketing. Any good marketing consultant will tell you to create a buyer persona (or avatar) so you can speak directly to your target audience with your marketing material. The same applies to recruiting. *Your employment brand is no different than your marketing brand.*

NEGATIVE PERSONAS

When you look at the ideal employee, you also have to know the qualities that make up the type of person you don't want on the team. This could include people who have no experience in customer service, do not have a particular degree, or had multiple errors on their resume (lack of attention to detail), etc.

Ironically, during the conversation, I referenced above (when the client had not exhausted their network for referrals), we determined that the person they thought they wanted for this role had never worked out in the past and there were a host of good reasons why.

It is important to identify your "non-negotiables" as a screening mechanism. For us, attention to detail is paramount. We will often leave a comment at the bottom of our job postings that states:

Please start your cover letter with: I have read and understood this job posting.

This helps us to screen out the candidates that are applying to every opening on the internet.

HOW TO CREATE AN EMPLOYEE PERSONA

You need to ask a lot of questions to paint the picture of the ideal employee persona. By the time you are done answering these, you will be able to see the people you want to hire. You will be able to articulate to friends and family who they should send your way.

Here are a few things you should ask and think about while developing an employee persona:

What kind of work experiences do top performers come from? What type of experience will they have (or not have)? What has their career path been? Are there specific industries that we are recruiting from? What kinds of things have they done or participated in to grow their knowledge in a position?

What are the characteristics of people who perform this role exceptionally well?

What are their professional mannerisms? What type of personality best suits this role? What are the interests of people that succeed in this type of position?

What goals does this type of person have?

Does the person who excels in this role have career goals? What are their primary goals? What are their secondary goals?

What motivates the person who excels in this role?

What are the influencers on their professional success? What are they motivated by? What do they care about?

How does this person behave?

In what communities would they be found? What does their network look like? What social activities are they involved in?

What compensation, education, and benefit offerings matter?

Does this person care about a career path? Are they focused on growth? Do they want to make an impact?

WHAT TO DO WITH THESE PERSONAS

By asking the above questions, you will have a clear picture of not only who you are looking for, but where they hang out, what matters to them, and how to construct a compelling employment offer. You can now become razor-sharp focused on your recruiting efforts.

REPEATABLE PROCESS

After identifying who you are looking for and where to look, you can establish a repeatable process that you can constantly use to develop bench strength. You should not only be recruiting when you have an opening.

When we know what we are looking for, we can ask better questions to determine if the person fits the mold. Ask questions that are aligned with the attributes you seek.

KEY POINTS TO REMEMBER

Don't Discriminate
Hire the right person.

Go Where They Are
Find your ideal fit.

Be Committed
Hire slow.

The persona is going to be one step in a multi-step process of finding the right people for your team. The below worksheet is used to help with the hiring process. We want to have total alignment between the Scorecard for the role, sourcing, performance management, and the duties being performed.

EMPLOYEE PERSONA DEVELOPMENT WORKSHEET

(find an electronic version of this at ergpayroll.com/book)

Background
What type of experience does the ideal candidate have? What industries have they worked in?

_____

_____

_____

Characteristics

What type of personality does the ideal person have? What are their personal and professional interests? What are their mannerisms?

_____

_____

_____

Motivations

What motivates this person? What are their career goals? What do they care about?

_____

_____

_____

Similar Personas

Who on your team or prior teams are like this person? How would you describe this person?

_____

_____

_____

THE RIGHT PEOPLE ARE KEY TO YOUR CULTURE

You cannot target the right type of people for your company and culture until you have an accurate representation of what they are. You need to use these employee personas the same way you would use a buyer persona to find the target customer.

Once you have created an employee persona for the role, we are going to move into finding the right candidates. The employee persona is the art and next is the science.

CHAPTER 4 TAKEAWAYS

We covered many topics about hiring in Chapter 4, but here are the main points to remember.

- If you don't know exactly what you are looking for, you won't find it.
- Bad hires can cost your company a fortune and are avoidable.
- Take the same approach as marketers by identifying an employee persona.
- Don't use personas as a tool to discriminate.
- Create a persona for any role that is either key to operations or that you will be hiring more than one person for.

CHAPTER 5:

SCREENING AND SELECTION

"Clients do not come first. Employees come first. If you take care of your employees, they will take care of the clients."
— **Richard Branson**

Hiring is not easy and finding talented people is harder than ever. Even when the supply has been higher in the past, the difference between "A" players and everybody else can mean the difference between businesses failing and staying open.

 Your culture is dependent on hiring the right people.

When you cut corners in the hiring process, the implications are so widespread they can sabotage you for years down the road. Studies from the Society for Human Resources Management (SHRM) suggest that every time a business replaces a salaried employee, the direct costs are 50-60 percent of an employee's annual salary. The total costs associated with a turnover range from 90-200 percent of annual salary.[5] If a teammate is making $40,000 a year, that's $20,000-$30,000 in direct expenses. That is a lot of dough.

But that's not the biggest problem. The ripple effect spreads further.

Think about it ...

You make a bad hire. You spend time and resources training that bad hire. They make mistakes. They piss off your clients. They piss off your team. They do things wrong and then show others the wrong way of doing things. Your customers leave. Your "A" players leave. You go from great to good.

---

[5]   *https://online.alvernia.edu/articles/cost-employee-turnover/*

Everything you have stayed up late at night to create and put your butt on the line for is risked because you just had to get someone hired right away and cut a few corners. *Was it worth it?*

These are the questions you must ask yourself before committing to the process below. It will take you much more time than you are used to. It will be hard. You will have positions open longer than you like. BUT you will hire "A" players at a much higher rate, which will have the exact opposite effect of what happens above. This is the new expectation.

You make a great hire. You spend less time training the new hire. They exceed expectations. They delight your clients. Your team loves to work together because they are around other "A" players. They create new and better ways of doing things. You get new customers. You grow and attract more "A" players. Your dream is alive.

When you know who you are looking for and can attract candidates, it is time to screen them. What does that mean? Think about a screen. Only the things you want to get through to the other side. Fresh air, sunshine, and a cool breeze. That is what we are doing here. Filtering out all the mosquitoes and letting the fresh air in. Remember, we are trying to build a culture that matters. That requires the right people in the right seats. You need to be diligent in this part of the process.

DO YOU THINK YOUR HIRING PROCESS IS LONG?

Bauknight, Pietras, and Stormer start their recruiting process in the fall for employees that will start during the fall of next year. They get about 20 candidates from the University of South Carolina (Go Cocks!) into the pipeline and whittle that down to ten, down to six, then down to four in the ideal recruiting class. These first 20 are already vetted and are top of their class. They will hire four of these candidates in October to start the following fall. All the while hoping that their final year does not go downhill and there are no changes in attitude. It is worth noting that these are graduate students who want to become CPA's. If you would have recruited me before one of my senior years, there is no telling what you would have got the next year. Once they accept the job, they might not start for eight months.

This is an incredibly long process compared to what most of us are used to. We have an open job right now and hope to fill the seat in 30 to 60 days! While there is no "right" amount of time to fill a job, it is important to take the time to do it right. You could find the right person and bring them through the process in a couple of weeks or it could take months. Be diligent and understand that a bad hire costs a lot more than an empty desk.

Below is a simple process you can implement at your company that will increase your hiring success rate by 25-50 percent *depending on your current process* (based on the success we have seen internally and with our clients). We will start with screening applicants through to reference checks. There are best practices you can take to make your current process better or you can use this system as your new system. You can always do more than this (sometimes people will add more interviews or time with the team or personal time with a candidate). The most important thing to remember is that you need to have a repeatable process and be disciplined in following it.

SCREENING OVERVIEW

Follow the below six steps when screening your candidates to identify the best fit for your organization. Remember, <u>do not skip any steps</u>.

Hire slow and find the right person for your team based on **evidence and facts**, not "gut."

<u>Six Steps</u>
1. Phone Screen
2. Skills Interview
3. Behavioral Interview

4. Team Interview

5. Reference Interview

6. Assessment

SCORING THE INTERVIEWS

Interviewing can be a nebulous process if you do not have a way to hold yourself accountable for hiring the right candidate for your team. It is important to have a scoring system in place that will help you to evaluate candidates' side by side after the shine of the interview wears off. This also helps to eliminate the halo effect. The halo effect occurs when one quality of a candidate shines over some of their less than stellar qualities. Use the below score sheet after each interview to make sure you are using a process that is based on reality, not just your memory.

You should grade the candidate after each interview and attach it to the employee file you are sharing with other interviewers (typically in an applicant tracking system). The applicant tracking system we provide to our clients at ERG Payroll & HR allows you to add collaborators to each job, track notes, grade the applicant right in the system, and makes this process very simple to automate. You can get a copy of this scoring sheet at *ergpayroll. com/book* and learn more about applicant tracking systems.

SCORING

Evaluate the candidate based on each of the qualities below. Use the numerical scale to grade how well the candidate represented each of these qualities. Provide any comments in the space given. Comments should indicate how thoroughly the candidate responded along with any potential concerns.

Candidate Name: _____ Position: _____ Interviewer Name: _____ Date: _____	**Rating** 1 - Poor 2 - Below Average 3 - Average 4 - Above Average 5 - Excellent
Educational Background: Does the candidate possess the appropriate education or training to perform the role at a high level?	
Comments:	
Prior Experience: Does the candidate have experience performing the requirements of the job or similar skills?	
Comments:	
Communication: Did the candidate demonstrate effective verbal (and non-verbal) communication skills during the interview?	
Comments:	
Preparation: Did the candidate show up with a printed resume show evidence of having prepared for the interview? Was the candidate on time?	
Comments:	
Coachable: Did the candidate answer questions in a way that proved they're open to constructive feedback from leaders?	
Comments:	
Team Player: Did the candidate demonstrate, through his or her answers, good interpersonal skills and refer to being part of a team?	

Comments:	
Technical Qualifications: Does the candidate have the technical skills or experience to succeed in this position?	
Comments:	
Initiative: Did the candidate demonstrate, through his or her answers, a high degree of initiative?	
Comments:	
Total:	
Grade: 32–40 = A 24–31 = B 16–23 = Do Not Hire	
Overall Impression and Recommendation: What are your recommendations for proceeding with the candidate?	

1. PHONE SCREEN

After you have compiled a group of potential candidates, you should spend 10-15 minutes on the phone with each of them to learn more about the candidate before making an investment of time. Don't ever set an in-person interview with someone you have not phone screened first.

Tips for setting up and performing phone interviews:

- Batch phone interviews to give you a good memory of the candidates.
- Limit the initial phone interview to 15 minutes.

- Have the interviewee's resume and the *Phone Interview Overview* (below) in front of you for the call.
- Be sure to explain any circumstances that might deter the candidate easily from the position; is it remote, part-time, a long drive from where they live, lower pay, high stress, etc.
- Do not commit to an in-person interview until you have interviewed all other candidates in that batch. <u>Do not schedule too many face-to-face interviews</u>. Use the scoring system to determine the best candidates.

Set up an in-person interview with *3-5 of the best candidates* for the position based on <u>score</u> (this can vary based on position and number of hires needed).

Initial Phone Screen Outline:

Thank you for taking the time to speak with us today. We would like to spend 15-20 minutes talking to see if the job is a good fit for both sides before we sit down for an interview. I wanted to ask you a few questions and share some information about the company. How does that sound?

Questions:

- Why did you apply for this position?
- What type of role are you currently looking for?
- Why are you currently searching for a new position?
- What are the top three duties in the job you have now, or in your most recent job that correlates well to the position we have posted?
- What do you know about our company?
- What are your long-term career goals?
- What are you good at professionally? Please give me some examples.
- What are you not good at or not interested in? Please give me some examples.

- Who were your last 5 bosses, and how will they each rate your performance when we talk with them (1-10)? Why?
- Is the salary range we have set for this position within your acceptable range?

Second-Level Questions: What, How, Tell Me More

After the candidate answers one of the questions, get deeper by asking follow-up "second-level" questions that begin with "What, How, or Tell Me More."

For example: *Say you asked the third question and they answered: "I want to find a position that will allow me to grow in my career."*

Simply say *"Tell me more about that" or "what does that mean" or "how do you plan to do that."*

Open-ended follow-ups allow the candidate to open up and give you more insight into the real answers.

Optional:

- Tell me about yourself.
- Why do you think you would be a good fit for this role?
- What has prepared you to be successful in this environment?
- What is your current salary and desired salary range?
- What are some typical decisions you make in your current role and how do you make them? Give some examples.

About Us:

Finish the call by explaining a little more about you, the role, and the company.

- Explain what you are looking for in the position.
- Explain any potential downside: Is the job part-time? far drive? low pay? small company?
- Discuss your mission and vision.
- Do you have any questions for me?

Close the conversation by letting them know you will be conducting in-person interviews next and you will contact them if they are invited. I always let applicants know that if they have not heard from me by X date, they can call me for a status update. This can act as a further screening method for some people if they are "on the fence."

2. THE SKILLS INTERVIEW

This is the first in-person interview and should last between 60 and 90 minutes.

You should ask questions about each of the last three to five positions they have on their resume working in chronological order. This will allow the candidate to explain their career as a story. Try to keep the candidate comfortable so they can open up. You can do this by being conversational, smiling, and being genuine. People can get very nervous during interviews. Do your best to be friendly as this will help them to get comfortable and share more valuable information with you. I have been in interviews where the interviewer was trying to stay profoundly serious and intimidate the interviewee. This does not help because the interviewee never takes their game face off and will not open up for you. They will mirror your behavior and are much more likely to show their real personality in a comforting environment.

Script to Open Interview:

Thank you for taking the time to come and see us today. The interview today will be mostly based on your prior roles in gaining an understanding of what you did and how you did it.

This interview can last anywhere from 30 minutes to two hours. I am going to ask you a set of questions around each role in chronological order for your last several positions.

We will review your skills and experiences and then allow you to ask me any questions you may have. At the end of the interview, we will discuss your career goals and aspirations and you will have the opportunity to ask me any questions.

While this sounds like a long interview, it will go remarkably fast. I want you to have the opportunity to tell your story.

How does that sound?

Skills-Based Questions

Ask these about each position:

Company Name/Role/Time in Role: _____

What accomplishments were you most proud of?	
Why did you choose this job?	
What would you have liked to do more of in that role? What held you back?	
Why did you/do you want to leave?	
• What was your boss's name, and how do you spell that?	
• What was it like working with him/her?	
• What will he/she tell me were your biggest strengths and areas for improvement?	
Systems or technology that were imperative to success in that role?	

Ask these as "general" questions:

- Why have you applied for this position?
- What skillset and value do you think you would bring to this position?
- What are your short-term and long-term professional goals?
- What do you know about our company?
- Why should we hire you?

- Now that you have learned about our company and the position for which you are applying, what hesitation would you have in accepting this job if we offer it to you?
- Tell me anything else you would like us to know about you that will aid us in making our hiring decision.
- What questions would you like to ask me?

If you are interested in the candidate, this is the time you should start qualifying their interest in the role and when they will be able to start if offered the position. You should also expand the "About Us" section below to start selling some of the benefits of working at your company (benefits, culture, pay, educational opportunities).

About Us:

At the end of the Skills Interview, go deeper into the "About Us" from the Phone Screen section and start to sell the company.

"A" Players will need to be sold on the position. How does the role align with their goals? What impact will this role have on their personal and professional goals?

Make sure you grade the interview using the Scoring Sheet above.

3. BEHAVIORAL INTERVIEW

The next step is an interview focused on the actual projects you have in mind for the candidate. This is the candidate's opportunity to prove that they are the best fit for the group. I would also suggest that you have multiple members of your team in the interview. This should include one of their potential teammates and anyone else who will be supervising them besides you.

Take an outcome you want out of the position from the job description. This is important. Don't focus on the task or less specific goals (grow sales)—focus on specific goals and how the candidate will approach them.

For example, one outcome might be "to grow sales 50 percent in year 1."

In that case, you might ask the candidate:

- What are some accomplishments you have in growing sales 50 percent or more?

- What are some mistakes and lessons you have learned in growing sales by 50 percent?

If another outcome you want is to lead the release of a major software product launch, then you ask the same types of questions about that.

At this point, you and the candidate are starting to envision the actual work you would be doing together, and the conversation should be quite natural.

BEHAVIORAL INTERVIEW OVERVIEW

The first portion of the interview should focus on outcomes. How will someone help you to achieve the desired outcomes of the role?

1. The purpose of this interview is to talk about _____ (one or more key outcomes or competencies).

2. What are some of the biggest accomplishments you have had in this area?

3. What are your biggest mistakes and lessons learned in this area?

The second portion of the interview should focus on behavioral and hypothetical situations.

Behavioral Questions

- Tell me about the best job you ever had? Why was it so good?

- Tell me about your short-term career goals? Why is this important to you?

- Tell me about your long-term career goals? Why is this important to you?

- Tell me about the type of people you like to work with? What are their characteristics? How do they work?
- Tell me about a time that someone pointed out that you had made an error. How did you react and what steps did you take to correct it?
- If someone asked you for assistance with a matter that is outside the parameters of your job description, what would you do, or how would you respond?
- Can you tell me about a time that this has happened and what was the result?
- You are a committee member and disagree with a point or decision made by another committee member. How will you respond? What actions will you take?
- Tell us about a time you dealt with conflict in the workplace.
- Tell me about a time when you were a part of a great team. What was your contribution and role in making the team effective?
- Give me an example of a time when you had to deal with a difficult co-worker. How did you handle the situation?
- Tell me about a personal or career goal that you have accomplished and why that was important to you.
- What strengths did you rely on in your current or last position to make you successful in your work?
- In your experience, have you ever been in a situation where a procedure or process that you were required to follow stated to do something one way, but you knew there was a better way to handle it? Can you tell me about the process and how you handled this conflict?
- Tell me about a time when one of the companies you worked for handed something down the chain of command (a policy, procedure, etc.) that you did not agree with? What did you do? How did you handle it?

- If you could write your job description, what would you be doing?

Core Values Related Questions

It is important to ask questions related to your Core Values. Your Core Values should be woven into your hiring process, performance management process, and day-to-day. They should always be top of mind. Here are some examples of questions you can add to the Behavioral Interview):

One of our Core Values is to provide support "Plus One" for our clients. This means anticipating their needs and going the extra mile to make sure they have everything they need to be successful. Can you give me an example of a time that you have embodied these characteristics in your work?

One of our Core Values is "Teamwork Makes the Dream Work." Tell me about a time you worked in a team environment and how you helped to bring the team together? What is your typical role when you are on a team?

Be conscious of the candidate's preparation and how well they align with the Core Values of the company. If they are not prepared, not dressed for success, or generally do not seem interested, proceed with caution. You are reviewing these answers to see how they align with the desired outcomes for the role. Do they have the experience or makeup to achieve what you are looking for?

Immediately after completion of the interview, rate the applicant based on the criteria you set out as important to the role. You will want to assign a letter grade so you can compare it against the other candidates. Put these grades in your notes.

Grade the interviewee. If they are not an "A" grade, they should not be moving forward.

4. THE TEAM INTERVIEW

It is especially important to get the potential teammate time with your people outside of the hiring managers. This could come in the form of a field ride, a "shadow day," a presentation to your team about why they are a good fit, dinner, or a couple of hours in the office interviewing your teammates to learn about the role. This step can vary greatly based on what you do (or the role) but should not be skipped. It can be formal or informal, but the time together is what matters most. As we mentioned earlier, anyone can act like a great teammate for a couple of interviews. You want to give them more time to let their guard down and show their true colors to your team.

You can also allow your team to do a panel interview for this portion of the process. This is highly suggested for roles that include a high amount of pressure and stress. There are very few things more stressful in life than a panel interview. You can see how someone prepares and performs under this level of pressure.

There are a lot of different ways to go during the team interview or team time portion of the interview process. This is a critical moment because you want to get as much time and exposure with your new potential teammate as possible. You also need to let your teammates know that it is ok to surface concerns about the candidate. Let them know that this is a large investment, and you value their opinions on whether this person will be a good fit for the job and the team.

5. REFERENCE INTERVIEW

It is time to ask others about the candidate. Call three to five references. Do not cut corners on this piece and do not let the reference off the hook with "they were great" and generic answers. Follow the script below:

Ask each reference the following questions:

1. In what context did you work with the person?

2. What were the person's biggest strengths? Please give me some examples.

3. What were some of the person's biggest areas for improvement back then? Please give me some examples.

4. How would you rate their overall performance in that job (1-10)?

5. The person mentioned that they struggled in that job with _____ (e.g. hitting their gross margin targets); tell me more about that.

Follow each step above (or more) in the process and **only hire someone who scores an "A"** in each step of the interview process. If you do not have any "A's," start over and engage a new flow of candidates.

Your team will thank you for being thorough when they have the good fortune of adding another "A" player to the team.

6. ASSESSMENTS

Before hiring someone, you should conduct several pre-hire assessments. You should conduct assessments to test their knowledge and skills, assessments to test their personality, and a background check.

Testing if someone has the skills or abilities for the job will help you to get a feel for if they are what they say they are. These assessments are particularly helpful in skilled positions like accounting or software development. If the position is one where the right person can learn the skills, you do not want to put too much weight on this assessment. Sometimes, hiring for attitude and aptitude is much more important than hiring for current skills.

Personality tests cause a lot of scrutinies but the right tests can give you great insight into a candidate's cognitive abilities, behavioral traits, and interests. Research conducted at the University of South Carolina[6] (*Go Cocks!*) suggests that many executive hires fail because of their behavioral and personality traits, not their ability to perform the job.

I love the PXT Select (a Wiley Brand) assessment. I recommend working with a certified partner. We have someone here in the Carolinas (Jim Fadell with Carolina Training and Assessments. Find more info at carolinatrainingandassessments.com). It is a thorough assessment that provides a high level of predictability of success for certain roles and personality types. While it is not the "end-all, be-all", it is another valuable piece of the candidate evaluation process.

Conducting a background check is a "no-brainer". Why wouldn't you want to know if you were hiring someone with a criminal background? It does not mean that you have to not hire them because of their background, it is just important to know. See the below statistics from National Crime Search:

- 50% of all resumes and applications contain false information
- 33% of all business failures are due to employee theft
- 18% of all violent crimes occur in the workplace

Wouldn't you want to know if someone had a history of behavior that you would not welcome before hiring them?

You must follow all state and federal regulations before performing any pre-hire assessment or using them in the decision-making process. You cannot perform assessments or background checks on someone without their permission and you cannot discriminate. For more information on the role of assessments in hiring decisions, check out our website, *ergpayroll.com*.

---

[6]   http://www.hrmagazine.co.uk/article-details/pat-wright-why-c-suite-hires-go-bad

CHAPTER 5 TAKEAWAYS

So, you have reached the point of screening potential candidates. Let's recap before moving on to employee onboarding.

- Not being thorough in your screening process can cost you thousands and destroy your culture.

- Being consistent with your process and grading will help you to screen out bad hires.

- Hire slow and fire fast. Do not make hires on "gut" decisions.

- Only hiring "A" players will take your company to the next level.

CHAPTER 6:

EMPLOYEE ONBOARDING

"You never get a second chance to make a first impression."
— Oscar Wilde

OK, so now you have found the right person for your team. The next critical component of building a culture of greatness is employee onboarding.

Researchers have found that the new hire onboarding process is a point in the employee lifecycle that has a tremendous impact on long-term success. Many of your employees know within the first ten days of employment whether they will be looking for another job in the next 18 months.

Every small business leader wants to get the most out of new team members as fast as possible—not to mention they want to retain them as members of the team. If that is the case, then why are so many companies missing a formalized onboarding process? What is it about the onboarding process that leads companies to make excuses for not having one in place?

The risk lies not in having an onboarding process, but not having an established program that helps your team members assimilate into your culture. If you want to have a team member who is engaged, productive, and likes their job, you need to have an onboarding process.

I am going to provide you with the resources and guidance needed to create an employee onboarding program that can be put on autopilot.

Sound good? Let's dive right in.

WHAT IS ONBOARDING?

Onboarding, also known as organizational socialization, refers to the mechanism through which new employees acquire the necessary knowledge, skills, and behaviors to become effective organizational members and insiders.

It has been proven, across large cross-sections of industries, that a formalized new hire onboarding process has an impact not only on employee performance but also on employee retention and engagement levels.

But there is so much more to onboarding than a detailed definition can provide. Ultimately, onboarding is a key step in getting your new hires acclimated to the current workplace culture—or the one you are in the process of creating. Learning the ins and outs of different office procedures is important but isn't the most essential. Take the time to make your onboarding process more than what is on a piece of paper.

WHAT IMPACT DOES ONBOARDING HAVE ON MY BUSINESS?

Attitudes and experiences within the first few days of employment shape how productive your new hire is at work—and how long they will stay at your company. <u>First impressions make a difference,</u> which is why a formal onboarding process is vital to employee retention.

Employee turnover is costly for employers, and the commitment level of employees to the organization can greatly impact profitability. When an organization can effectively onboard and assimilate team members, turnover will go down.

If your company has a high turnover and you do nothing to solve the issue, the repercussions could be awfully expensive. Constantly replacing employees, poor morale among your team members, and high training costs could run you up as much, if not more, than providing a new employee with a solid onboarding experience.

As a company leader, you are trying to remain competitive. It takes top talent to do that. If your team members are constantly changing and you can't retain your "A" players, how can you expect to stay ahead of your competition? Think about the fallout you experienced when a team member left your organization. What action was taken as a result? What sorts of things did you learn from that experience? Use what you learned to write the kind of onboarding process you would want to be a part of.

IS THERE A SOLUTION?

No one way is guaranteed to decrease employee turnover, but several strategies can be carried out to make a positive impact on the future of your team.

By implementing a formalized employee onboarding process, you can expect to see a decrease in turnover **and** an increase in employee engagement. The achievement of decreased turnover is a result of the socialization process helping new employees become members of your team sooner.

So, how do you reach a possible solution for your team?

Combine a formalized process with the right technology and you will have a solid framework for reducing employee turnover and making your people more productive.

WHY IS ONBOARDING THE KEY?

The new hire onboarding process has been proven to have a direct correlation to each of the performance indicators. Companies that have formalized onboarding processes see about 60 percent year-over-year improvement in productivity versus those that do not have one.

Do you know when a new hire makes their first impression of your organization? It is during the new hire onboarding process. This is the ideal opportunity to develop a relationship with a new team member that can either be highly productive and engaged or "just another job." This relationship may enhance employees' commitment levels, which are important and should be established early on through proper new hire processes.

The formalization of assimilation and socialization of new hires as part of the onboarding process has proven to increase the speed at which employees achieve performance milestones. Higher operational performance can also be expected at organizations that have more progressive HR practices, like mentor programs, which we will talk about in Chapter 7. All in all, when employees feel more comfortable in their work environment, it will lead to greater employee output, and that is why onboarding is key.

CREATING AN EMPLOYEE ONBOARDING PROGRAM

Define the goals of your onboarding program

This is the most important part:
    You need to have goals. I repeat. You need to have goals.

Sample Goals for Onboarding Program:
- Improve employee retention by 15 percent
- Improve customer satisfaction survey scores by 5 percent
- Reduce labor costs by 5 percent

Once you have set your goals, there are three main areas that you need to focus on when creating your organization's onboarding program:
- Education and Training
- Assimilation/Socialization
- Documents/Tasks

EDUCATION AND TRAINING

Teaching someone how to do a job effectively and setting proper expectations is something that most companies struggle with. The biggest mistake that many small business owners make when establishing an onboarding program for their employees is not setting a defined goal or having a goal that is poorly defined.

You may set goals like "sell more" or "have better customer service," but the lack of definition and specificity can and will be your downfall.

The target should not only be measurable, like increasing sales by 10 percent for Product A or improving employee retention by 25 percent, but the onboarding program should give team members the training and resources needed to reach those goals.

How can you measure this progress?

- Knowledge tests
- Oral interviews
- Training completion

ASSIMILATION/SOCIALIZATION

Assimilation into a new organization affects more than just the happiness and productivity of a single employee. When employees are not onboarded properly, it can affect those around them and the profitability of the entire company. By finding ways to better assimilate new hires, organizations will help to increase their productivity and reduce employee turnover. The key to assimilating new hires into your culture is to submerge them in it from the get-go.

How can you measure this progress?

- Team trivia
- Scavenger hunt
- Mentor program

MENTOR PROGRAMS

An additional method of dealing with the challenges of employee turnover is to create mentor programs as part of the new hire onboarding process. Mentor programs have been proven to help develop more productive employees. Organizations could make it a requirement for every employee, regardless of tenure or position, to have a mentor at work.

A mentor could provide a new hire with assistance on improving work-related skills—all while helping them assimilate into the workplace culture. Put yourself in a new hire's shoes: Your mentor should not be able to fire you. As a company leader, it is your job to match mentors with new hires. Work can sometimes be a lonely place, and it helps to have an advocate or mentor both personally and professionally. Mentor programs will be covered more in-depth in Chapter 7.

DOCUMENTS/TASKS

There will always be a list of documents and tasks that need to be completed by new hires before their first day or during the first week at work. These items will vary based on your organization but could include reading the employee handbook, completing a direct deposit form, or signing a confidentiality agreement. Remember to have a checklist that makes it easier for you to follow up with new hires while being consistent and compliant with federal laws.

How can you measure this progress?

- Track completion in an onboarding system.
- Review progress of new hire documents with a mentor on day three of employment.
- Meet with a new hire at the end of their first week to discuss documents or tasks.

PREPARING FOR A NEW HIRE'S FIRST DAY

When you fail to prepare, you are preparing yourself to fail—and that directly relates to your organization's onboarding process. We talked about how important first impressions are for new hires, so make your preparations beforehand to ensure new hires receive a warm welcome on their first day. Take advantage of a new hire's first day by showing them all that your organization has to offer for their career goals and expectations. I have included a pre-hire checklist to give you a head start on preparing for a new hire's first day.

Pre-Hire Checklist

- Plan the new hire's first project.
- Put recurring 1:1 meetings with management on the calendar.
- Set up their computer, install software, and other accessories.
- Set up the new hire's email.
- Add the new hire to relevant email lists.
- Set up their work area with supplies, company swag, etc.
- Get keys or codes—items that are necessary to enter the organization.
- Select a mentor for the new hire.
- Communicate the new hire's general info, like name and incoming role, and share with your entire team.
- Encourage your team to reach out to the new hire.
- Provide new hires with a start date and time.
- Send over info about the organization's dress code.

Take a moment to think about your current pre-hire checklist or process. What are three things about it that you would change today? Your organization's onboarding process should be modified over time—staying up to date will keep your team on the cutting edge, especially when it comes to hiring and onboarding.

THE FIRST DAY

A new hire's first day is an emotional and memorable day that you can capitalize on if completed properly. How you prioritize the first-day process for new hires says a lot about your company as a whole. If you prioritize going over rules and paperwork but forget the introductions and assimilation with other employees, what does that say about your priorities? Every little detail matters on the first day, which is why it is crucial to follow a pre-hire checklist as I mentioned previously.

The first day should be spent delivering an experience to your new hire. Capture the hearts and minds of your entire team by covering your real priorities, like teamwork, clients, brand promise, mission, and company values. Talk about *how* things get done, not necessarily *what* gets done.

Imagine that you were just rehired at your organization. What would the perfect first day look like? What would you do, learn, and experience?

Take your ideas about the perfect first day and make changes to your process to ensure your vision is fulfilled. In addition to creating an agenda for your new hire's first day, make one for yourself. This will ensure you remain accountable for making their experience as close to perfect as it can be.

So, what are some things that should be covered on a new hire's first day?

- Your organization's core values
- Your vision
- Your brand promise
- Your team
- What to expect during the next 90 days

TRAINING PROGRAMS

Training assets are a vital component of any onboarding process. How you train new hires and provide consistent training to tenured team members reflects your company's Core Values. Think about the skills of the employees who embody your Core Values. What is it about the way they perform their jobs that would help in creating different training strategies for others?

Every employee learns and trains in a unique way, which is why you should have different types of training that you execute regularly. These pieces of training could include role play, games and simulations, mentoring, job rotation, and computer-based training. By analyzing the effectiveness of your current training strategies, you can determine the new mechanisms that would be beneficial to your team's performance.

Ask yourself these three questions before deciding on a training program for your organization. These questions will help you shine a light on the ideals and values that are most important to your organization's future.

- What training do you wish you would have received during your first three months of employment?
- What was the most memorable or useful training that you received since starting at your organization?
- What is the most important skill to being successful at your organization?

The key to creating a training program that sticks is by following up with new hires and reinforcing the training received by doing routine check-ins or quizzes. I would like to make a note here as a reminder to ask your new hires what types of things they would like to learn during a training program. Of course, they need to learn the inner workings of your organization, but you should also be tapping into their interests to make sure they get the most out of their training.

SETTING MILESTONES IN THE ONBOARDING PROCESS

First Week

Test the new hire on first-day knowledge. Why does their role exist? What do we stand for? What is our mission?

You can do this at a 1-week check-in meeting, which should focus on gathering the new hire's initial feedback and satisfaction with their onboarding program.

30 Days

During their first week of employment, define the goals that a new hire should accomplish within 30 days. Determine three strong goals that can be measured and are related to their role or position at your organization.

For example:

- Complete 5 payrolls with little oversight.
- Complete 6 hours of HR training.
- Lead a team meeting.

Have another check-in meeting with the new hire to determine progress and adjust 60-day goals as necessary. Some team members will be ahead, which is great. If they are behind, identify why and how to fix it. Ask lots of questions at these meetings. Also, be sure to check-in with each new hire's mentor to see how you can help.

60 Days

Define the goals that an employee should have completed by the end of 60 days. Use the same process as you did for 30 days.

90 Days

Review the employee Scorecard (See page 131). Grade the employee against the competencies and establish goals for the next

90 days that will help the employee to improve on key competencies and achieve the outcomes for the year.

6 Months

Execute a survey of what the new hire remembers from their first 90 days. Look for trends to emphasize or de-emphasize what is working. Evaluate the new hire's performance against Scorecard Outcomes and measure the performance in key competencies.

1 Year

Have defined goals for the role at the 1-year mark. These should be outlined in the Scorecard before making the hire.

CHAPTER 6 TAKEAWAYS

Let's reflect on what we learned in Chapter 6 about the importance of employee onboarding.

- You only have one chance to make a first impression.
- The impact of a properly conducted and formal new hire onboarding process impacts engagement, retention, and productivity.
- Employee onboarding is proven to have the biggest impact on retention and engagement.
- You need processes in place to make sure that employees have a great experience.
- Make sure your onboarding program extends beyond the point of hire and into education and performance management.

CHAPTER 7:

EMPLOYEE TRAINING AND DEVELOPMENT

*"All growth depends upon activity.
There is no development physically
or intellectually without effort,
and effort means work."*
— **Calvin Coolidge**

I often ask people what their new hire training program looks like and they respond with something along the lines of "baptism by fire" or "we learn by doing" or "drinking from a fire hose." It seems to be a badge of honor for companies to *not* have a training program. It is a shame.

One of the most sought-after qualities in a new company for job seekers is how good their education and training program is. If you are not willing to invest in the development of your people, someone else will be. Even worse, if you don't invest in them, they will stay, take up a seat and "just get by."

Training goes far beyond teaching people how to do the job at your company. How the widgets are made is only one piece of what it takes to be successful in the workplace and be a highly contributing member of an awesome culture. There are a host of things that people need to continue to develop professionally, including everything from how to communicate effectively, how to stay organized, and time management. Improper education and training of your people mean poor delivery of your product or service that equates to customers leaving or having to reproduce work when your team makes errors and mistakes.

Just behind a competitive wage, millennials rank excellent training and development programs as one of the most important characteristics of an attractive employer[7]. Training is more than just improving performance. It is about keeping and engaging your talent.

Check out this excerpt from an article in *Training* magazine:

Research by John Kotter and James Heskett makes the financial argument. They conducted an 11-year study comparing the performance of 12 companies that had an adaptive culture with 20 companies that did not. Companies with adaptive cultures outperformed the competition by a tremendous margin:

Average increase for 12 firms with performance-enhancing cultures

Average increase for 20 firms without performance-enhancing cultures

Revenue Growth

With: 683 percent

Without: 166 percent

Wow. What a difference it made for companies that are willing to include training as part of their company culture. You can't logically argue that companies who are focused on learning and getting better are not only going to have a better culture but are going to produce stronger results. It just makes sense.

IS TRAINING THE ISSUE?

Let me paint a picture for you of a common interaction I have with clients: "We just need a better training program. We have been marching down this path for quite a while and getting anyone to commit time to this better training program is getting harder by the day." The clients are often adamant about making a change but don't put in the effort to refurbish or redesign their current training protocol.

A new hire's entire career at a company begins with training. If the training program is lackluster and provides nothing but the

---

7   https://www.pwc.com/gx/en/industries/financial-services/publications/millennials-at-work-reshaping-the-workplace-in-financial-services.html

basics, how can a company expect to have high employee engagement and performance? When people are not performing at the expected level, it is easy to say training is the issue. Creating a great training program is hard. Before you commit to training on any process, you need to make sure that training is the issue.

Training can help with three main issues: a gap in skill, a gap in ability, or a knowledge gap. But Matt, isn't this pretty much everything? No! If your employees do not have the right tools, equipment, software, or materials to do their job, then training is not going to fix that.

You need to put people in an environment to succeed and then train them on how to do the job right.

Make sure that any performance issues you are looking at are related to employees not having the knowledge, skills, or ability to do something. If they have those things but don't have the tools, or you don't have the processes in place, take a step back and work on the processes first.

DEVELOPING A TRAINING PROGRAM

Creating a training program for your company is not easy, but it does not have to be complicated either. There are a handful of critical elements to keep in mind as you start to create a training program for your team.

First of all, start with the fundamentals. Train your team on the things that every employee at your company will need to know. In some organizations, this means how to properly greet a customer, operate a piece of software or a piece of equipment, or how to deliver an effective "elevator pitch" about the company. There are many famous organizations, like Zappos, that will make their employees cross-train across almost every department before going into their role so they can have a full-scale view of the organization.

In most circumstances, you would like to have your employees shadow other departments, but you want to handle the fundamentals first. This can include how to communicate things internally, what your product offerings are, how they are made and sold, and everything about your company at a high level so employees know "how the sausage is made."

The most overlooked training that every small business should spend time training their people on is *effective communication*. Communication is the most critical element of success and failure in a high-performing team. In an environment where communication can take on many forms (email, text, chat, and more), it's important to train your team on how to properly communicate with one another. This includes not only how to engage with teammates but how to properly deliver and receive information. Think about all the ways you are going to need your team to communicate; projects, sharing work-related information, how to take and deliver feedback, and more. Proper communication is the bedrock of a great culture.

There are many great pieces of training on the internet (we use Lynda.com) and books on how to improve team communication. Whenever we do an employee survey in a low-performing culture, communication is one of the biggest complaints from employees. They complain that they do not know what's going on and that communication across teams and departments is poor. As soon as you have people, you will have communication issues. It is important to spend time creating training and policies to help create the type of environment where people communicate as effectively as possible.

Another example of a "baseline" piece of training that all teammates could need would be how to use the internal systems that nearly every employee uses. At our company, almost every employee will interact with our Customer Relationship Management (CRM) tool at some point. We want to make sure they know what the CRM is and how to utilize it in their first few weeks. The same goes for our document management software. How do you interact with your filesharing system? Do you have an Intranet or some other core document management system? Create training that can impact almost every type of employee that walks through your door. This will help you to create a foundation or bedrock for success that your organization can use to fine-tune your training process.

UNDERSTANDING THE TRAINING YOUR TEAM NEEDS

One of the best ways to understand what training your team needs is to survey them. This is the most overlooked and obvious component of creating a training program. Ask your employees what they wish they had more training on. You can also ask managers for areas where their team could use improvement. The feedback you receive from your team, management, and the internal metrics will help you to prioritize what types of training you should create first and who should be involved in those training. The next thing you want to understand is how you will deliver the training.

There are so many different methods to deliver training it can be difficult to choose one that's right for your team. If you are a small company, oftentimes you can find external resources to do that you can supplement with your team. For example, we use Lynda.com for training on everything from how to improve sales skills to customer service, Excel, and beyond. We improve this training by stopping to watch the recording together and then stopping again to talk through different ideas or topics using the resource materials. Delivery is crucial when it comes to conveying information to every person on your team. There are three types of learners: visual, audio, and kinesthetic.

Visual: This type learns by seeing. Videos, in-person meetings, social media posts—anything that involves this learner to see and process information using their eyes.

Audio: This type learns by hearing. Podcasts, video seminars, informative phone interviews—this learner takes what they hear and turns it into an idea or solution.

Kinesthetic: This type learns by physical activity. Think of the expression, "Learn by doing." This type of learner dives right into a project or training program that requires their action.

If you create a training program that only appeals to one or two out of the three learners, you will be losing a large portion of your audience. It is critical to design your training to meet the needs of each learner. There should be a visual component, this could be a video or speaker with slides. There should be an audio component.

In other words, I should be able to hear somebody speak about what is happening and how to perform the task or skill that I'm trying to learn. There should be a hands-on component, like role-play or a behavior modeling situation. When you combine each of these elements, you have a much higher likelihood of success with your training program.

WHAT MAKES ONE SMALL BUSINESS BETTER THAN ANOTHER?

When I talked with Shawn Regan about their training program, he put it to me like this: "The first thing that makes us successful is that, for a small business, we have one. It is something that we continue to try to work on". Wow. It starts there, simply with having a training program. It is amazing how many small businesses do not even have a training program for their employees. The leadership team often expects others to train them on how to do the job with no resources or methods to the madness.

Here is more of what Shawn had to share regarding their education and training program:

"For the last few years, we have had company goals around being a "Best Place to Work" and to improve people's lives (purpose of the company). To help us with attracting and retaining top talent, we have embarked on creating a management training course, a business course. We use an outside consultant who is helping us create these three courses that anyone can take for when they are moving into internal management roles".

People who are being promoted into leadership positions that have never been a manager before seem to be one of the "lowest hanging fruit" opportunities when developing a training program. Expecting people to just jump in and be a good manager is not going to happen. Nobody ever takes a class or learns how to interview someone, same with management, if you have never managed, how do you handle that?

IDENTIFYING TRAINING NEEDS

I was meeting with the leadership team of a company with about 60 employees. There were about 10 of us around a table and one thing everyone knew was that the training program needed to be improved. It was something the employees mentioned, and all of the leaders agreed on. Now came the difficult part; what do we need to train people on and how? There were about 15 different positions in the company that all had unique responsibilities and skills required.

 How could we create a program that helped everyone and met the needs of the company?

We sat around a U-shaped set of tables in their conference room, that looked like a training room, debating what the first steps should be. I started asking questions about what they already have in place and what the desired outcomes of the program would be. There were varying ideas about what a good program looked like, what training was needed, who needed it, and how to execute. There was even one person defending the existing training since they had created it.

As with all leadership teams, there were strong personalities and rarely a consensus. Eventually, we came to a majority that I could start to lead the conversation since that was what I was there for and something I had done hundreds of times. I walked them through the process we are going to follow below. This process works whether you have 6 or 60 employees in your company or department. The structure is built and can be used to create a single training class or a program for an entire company.

Start with the end in mind

The first thing you need to understand is the goal of implementing the training program. When you are first starting, it should be to deliver your product or service. As your program moves forward, it can be about increasing efficiency, top-line growth or bottom-line growth, or even increasing employee retention. There are a lot of things that can be accomplished in implementing a training program, but it's important to have one single goal to start. The desired impact will improve the performance of the business. That includes the level of performance the learners must be able to reach to create the impact, along with the knowledge and skills they need to learnto perform. These desired outcomes will help guide all decisions on how to structure the training.

Sample Goals

- Improve sales by 10 percent
- Reduce turnover by 10 percent
- Improve customer satisfaction rating by 5 percent

The main goal we were trying to accomplish at this aforementioned company was to decrease employee turnover. This was a great goal and allowed us to focus our efforts when developing the training program. It was also a "domino goal." In other words, once this goal was accomplished, other things would be easier to complete. This goal acted as the lead domino. If we reduced turnover and had higher-performing employees that stayed with the company longer, we would be able to achieve many of the company's other objectives, like reducing overhead and expanding into new markets. It also aligned well with what we were hearing

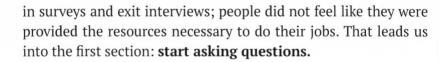

in surveys and exit interviews; people did not feel like they were provided the resources necessary to do their jobs. That leads us into the first section: **start asking questions.**

Ask questions

What are the training needs and what will success look like? This question should be asked in many ways and to multiple stakeholders inside and outside of the organization. This includes managers, employees, clients, and vendors. Everyone who interacts with your team. I often see companies skip this and just start implementing what the leaders think needs the most attention.

The "needs" assessment will typically identify common themes and areas of improvement that will have a direct impact on organizational success. It is important to gain perspective from multiple sources, including the employees, to learn where you have the best opportunity for impact. We want to get feedback from all stakeholders, including employees, managers, and executives.

We have created this simple format for gathering feedback that allows you to not only understand some of your training needs but what you might already have in place that you were unaware of. Have your leadership team and employees complete this (if you have more than 25 employees on the team, choose a few who have been there for a long time and some that are newer).

EMPLOYEE DEVELOPMENT QUESTIONNAIRE

What are three goals you have for your self-development?

_____

_____

_____

Who are three people you have worked with that embody the qualities that will allow you to reach those goals?

1. _____

2. _____

3. _____

What are the characteristics of these people?

_____

_____

_____

What skills do these people possess?

_____

_____

_____

What are the characteristics of poor performers you have worked with?

_____

_____

_____

Please circle the types of training we have here and rate how well they were executed on a scale of 1-10

- On-the-Job Training _____
- Role Playing _____
- Self-Instruction _____
- Games and Simulations _____
- Computer-Based Training ____
- Mentoring _____
- Job Rotation _____
- Performance Appraisal _____
- Classroom _____

What training classes or programs have you participated in? *(Please note how the training is administered from the examples above)*

_____

_____

_____

_____

_____

_____

_____

_____

_____

_____

_____

_____

_____

_____

_____

What trainings do we not currently offer that you believe are a need?

_____

_____

_____

_____

_____

_____

_____

_____

_____

_____

_____

_____

Which training that we offer is the most effective?

_____

_____

_____

_____

What training do you wish you would have received during your initial three months of employment here?

_____

_____

_____

What was the most memorable and useful training you have received since starting here?

_____

_____

If you could only complete one training during your first week, what would it be?

_____

What is the most important skill to being successful here?

_____

Please rate the below competencies and their importance to being successful here.

(*Note: You are going to see this list of competencies throughout the book. That is because once you identify the competencies that are important to your company, you can use them to evaluate candidates, measure performance, improve your training program, and more. Spend time finding out what is important to your team.*)

1 is least important and 5 is most important.

Competency	Importance (1-5)	Notes
Quality: The extent to which an employee's work is accurate, thorough, and neat.		
Productivity: The extent to which an employee produces a significant volume of work efficiently in a specified period of time.		
Attendance and Punctuality: The extent to which an employee adheres to established work schedules and is timely for meetings or other scheduled visits or appointments with clients, employees, and/or applicants.		
Job Knowledge: The extent to which an employee possesses the practical/technical knowledge required on the job.		
Training Effectiveness: The extent to which an employee can grasp new ideas, methods or concepts, the speed of learning and retention.		
Communication: The extent to which an employee demonstrates written and verbal communication skills.		
Initiative: The extent to which an employee seeks out new assignments and assumes additional duties when necessary.		

Competency	Importance (1-5)	Notes
Interpersonal Relationships: The extent to which an employee is willing and demonstrates the ability to cooperate, work, and communicate with coworkers and supervisors.		
Service Relationships: The extent to which an employee is willing and demonstrates the ability to cooperate, work and communicate with clients, applicants, and employees, and successfully builds rapport with them.		
Dependability: Reliability in following through on assignments and instructions.		
Judgment: The extent to which an employee demonstrates proper judgment and decision-making skills when necessary.		
Professionalism: The extent to which an employee represents the company in a professional manner, including interactions with others, quality of work, and representation of the company both in the office and in public.		

Once you receive the questionnaires back, it is time to review what you have and begin to put together a list of the core competencies and critical skills necessary to succeed at your company. You are looking for common themes. Do things like communication, system knowledge or sales techniques come up the most frequently? What groups of your company need the most help?

What stage of the employee lifecycle are people struggling with the most and when should that be addressed?

Now that we have identified our needs, we need to try to tackle the biggest domino first. Which of these skills or competencies will improve the others AND impact the goal of the training program the most? For example: if our goal from above was to improve sales by 10 percent and we found during our survey that our team had a lot of issues with understanding our CRM system, we might start with pipeline management and how to effectively use our sales tools. We might also begin to train them on how to properly ask for referrals or run sales meetings—it really depends on the other answers.

We can follow this order below with the above tools to get a baseline for our program in place:

- Identify core competencies and critical skills
- Develop list of available trainings
- Identify avenues to fill knowledge gaps

Once we have completed the questionnaire, we will have a ranked list of our core competencies and critical skills along with some feedback on what training worked well and the opportunity to identify trends in training needs. After we finish steps one and two, we can start to identify avenues to fill knowledge gaps.

PREPARING TO ROLL OUT TRAINING

This is the most important step. The team needs to identify the method of training, the people who will be involved, and the goals of the training. This is when you will define what success looks like. Is it attainable and how can we get there? Give your people the resources they need to execute and make the learning an ongoing process rather than a one-time event.

Small business leaders usually fail to make sure *everyone* is prepared for the training. This includes the employee, the trainers, and the employees' manager. The training will fall flat if the manager or team has not bought off on the *need* for the education and therefore does not give ample support to the employee or commitment to taking what they have learned and applying it. This can result in the benefits being minimized by a lack of focus and unwillingness to take it seriously. Take the time to gain support from both the team and leadership to educate them of the desired results and how that will contribute to the team's success.

EXECUTION

Whatever your method and plan are, make sure you stick to it. Give your team the time to execute without feeling the pressure of tying up resources. When the trainers are trying to rush material or minimize the content (they are making it feel unimportant as they are teaching), they can minimize the impact of the whole process. As with every great plan in business, it all boils down to execution. We talked about this earlier. You do not have to get "A's" across the board, but you better get at least a "B-" in every discipline of culture. Do not confuse this with the hiring process (only hire "A" players), when it comes to all of the disciplines discussed in this book. You don't have to be a pro at everything, but you definitely have to be doing all of it at a "B-" level or higher. Always link the training directly to the job being performed and provide exercises that will not only keep the trainee involved, but actively learning.

 You do not have to get "A's" across the board, but you better get at least a "B-" in every discipline of culture.

MEASURING THE EFFECTIVENESS OF TRAINING

It is time to identify if the training stuck. The goal of training is to improve performance and maximize productivity. There are several different ways to measure the effectiveness of the training. The result should involve measuring trainee satisfaction, knowledge tests, performance improvements, and ROI metrics. These "measurables" were defined in the planning stage and can now be assessed to determine the stickiness of the program and allow for future enhancements. Do not skip this step as it is the most important piece of the puzzle. If you do not have a way to measure your goal from the first step, that should be part of this process—find a way to measure it!

DIFFERENT METHODS OF TRAINING

It was one of the more complicated training manuals I have ever seen, but I must admit, I was impressed. They were an electrical company and a seemingly "normal" company compared to others in the industry, but I started to realize they were not normal.

"I want every one of my guys doing exactly the same thing at every job," he told me as we looked at their workflow on several large whiteboards on the wall in their large warehouse. The whiteboards had drawings that showed everything that must be done from the time someone set foot on a job site. It was a thing of beauty.

"We have really high turnover in this industry, and I want to be able to hand people the playbook on day one. I don't want them doing it the way they did it at their old company, I want it done our way."

Not only did they have a strong process for training people "their way" from the day they were hired, but they were also committed to the continual learning of their teammates. They would send teammates to offsite trainings and pay them more when they received certifications or additional training. This truly was the type of culture that promoted learning and wellbeing. The employees appreciated it and they looked the part. They were clean-cut, took a lot of pride in their work and were almost boastful of how much better electricians they were than the competition.

There are five ways we can train our people.

- Internal training
- Online training
- Courses or seminars
- External training companies
- College or university

Depending on the training need, each serves its purpose. Let's take a deeper dive into each type of training and provide some resources to help you develop your program.

Creating internal training

Money spent on training can be one of the best investments your company makes, or a huge waste of time and capital. The outcome is almost completely controllable, and the difference lies in the execution. If you do not have the desired result that can be measured and tracked, do not spend a dollar. The goal should not be poorly defined as "sell more" or "have better customer service." The target should be measurable (i.e., increase sales by 10 percent for product A) with training that allows you to attain it as we defined above.

Training also does not have to be some grand act of commitment that includes a three-part training module and workshop for everything your company does. Below we are going to talk through how to develop training for some of the most mundane things you do and the most important things you do. There are many occasions where a simple recording of your screen, while you are performing a task or a Google Doc, can handle what you need. Those are **tasks**. When you are talking about changing behavior, you need to train **competencies**.

Internal training can take several forms. We want to use a little of each of these to get the right formula.

One-on-One Training: This is an informal process where one employee sits down with another and explains how to use a piece of software or complete a certain business process. This is probably the most common form of training that takes place in small businesses.

Presentations/Lunch and Learns: This is where teammates who are subject matter experts or leaders share information. This could either be a formal presentation or an informal gathering over lunch or coffee.

Mentoring: A mentor program is about much more than just training, but often there is an element of training to it. A mentor will often pass on important skills, tips and advice to the person being mentored. Mentor programs are proven to help in the engagement and retention of employees. I suggest pairing up mentors after a teammate has been with you for 30 days so that you can make sure the people will be a "match" and both get a lot out of the relationship.

If you really want to see the effectiveness of your training rise, you should always have a measurable goal, even for individual training. For example: if you are trying to decrease the time your nurses take to capture a blood sample you could have individual training focused on helping each person get better. After extra training course X, Nurse Sally should decrease her time in taking a blood sample by 50 percent in the three months following the course.

Using the employee development questionnaire

Taking the information from the survey, we have created our list of core competencies and critical skills that we need to train for. These are not the only things that matter, just the ones that matter the most. See our answers below:

- Quality
- Dependability
- Initiative
- Interpersonal Relationships
- Service Relationships

These critical skills translated into a host of different training opportunities, like learning our internal operating systems, customer service fundamentals, how to be an effective teammate, and so on. We started to identify what skills fell into these competencies by looking back at the survey results from the questions like, "What training do you wish you received in the first three months?" and "What was the most memorable training you have received since starting here?" to connect the dots. Now we had a clear picture of where we were missing training. You might be asking, "How do you train initiative?" It is important that your training aligns with your expectations and what it takes to get the job done. While you might not be able to train initiative into someone, you can certainly create the right expectations and environment for them to be able to move forward without support or roadblocks when it is time to get the job done. You can also train people on how to overcome adversity, which is a big part of being able to show initiative. As you can see, there are a lot of ways to develop your people to the competencies that matter most to your company.

Next up, we took what we already had available and cataloged it so it is easy to find. We use a system called Zoho Connect that has a "manuals" section. We create manuals for all of the core competencies of our company. Now we want to make sure that we have decided which of the above and below methods is the best way to train for the skill.

For example: Part of our Service Relationships Critical Skills is the ability to communicate with the IRS. Showing someone how to submit a report to the IRS is probably best done with one-on-one and manual training. Whereas keeping up with legal requirements for human resources is something that we would want to do with external partners. Whichever type of the three training methods we do above, we try to develop a written process for it.

As with many small businesses, we have turnover, particularly with our interns, who by nature aren't hired with the intention of long-term employment. However, hiring an intern could be a great way to test out a potential new hire over a period. It could also be the ideal opportunity to see how well a training program works. We have created videos, tutorials, and manuals on how to do many of the basic tasks that our interns will be doing. Although their workload may not be as intense as full-time employees, interns do not typically require one-on-one training, so having a program lined up could be beneficial to you—and to them.

Allowing employees to teach

By giving your team members the opportunity to teach the rest of the team about skills and processes that they are good at, you will build confidence in the employee, bolster their knowledge, and educate your team. This is a huge win for everyone involved.

Once you start to identify training needs, you can find the people on your team that are best at these skills and allow them to create training for the team as a stretch assignment.

You should create a framework for how to develop and lead the training. You are most likely going to be leaning on people who have never formally developed a training class before. A simple checklist would be helpful. Here is an example of one you could use.

Resources

- **Snagit**—Record your screen and talk over it. This is great for things that are done at a computer and are more task-based than competency based. When you are small, creating videos of how you do things takes only a few extra minutes, but can save you from ever having to do that task again as your company grows and your time is less.

- **Zoho Connect**—Connect is fantastic for creating standard operating procedures and acting as the "Library" for all of your training material. We have manuals and articles for nearly everything we do, including access to our outside training material (vendor websites and course catalogs) in our Training Manual.

- **Google Drive**—Creating a good folder system and using Docs, Slides, and Sheets will allow you to document most of your systems and share access with your team in real time. No more keeping up with different versions as things change as Google updates in real time.

Online training

Often, people think it is too expensive to use outside training for their small business. At ERG Payroll & HR, one of the most valuable training tools we use almost weekly is free. That is right. Free. Tens of thousands of course on everything ranging from communication and time management, to software development, leadership, coaching, and everything in between.

This resource is *Lynda.com* (recently acquired by LinkedIn). We get it for free with our library membership and use it with our team. You can also purchase access to the training library through their website, Lynda.com. We can create learning tracks for specific roles and do training together as a team or individually. We stop the videos and talk about how it applies to us, as well as take notes and tack action items that we can use to improve. There are also valuable resource materials for most classes. This tool has been invaluable for us. We have catered an online resource to all learning styles by doing the group trainings where we stop, talk, and create during the session.

If you search your industry and training classes online, you will likely find resources that apply to you. The most critical step is to put a process around why, when, and how people will be required to complete these training sessions. This should be infused into onboarding and part of the annual learning plan.

Courses or seminars

Getting out of the office and going to a course or seminar for even a few hours can be refreshing to your teammates. There is also an emotional component of learning offsite in a new place that helps to anchor some of the information retained. There are a host of other things you can do for you and your employees when it comes to learning outside of the office.

You can enroll in associations that are specific to your industry. For example: Our HR Business Partners belong to the local chapter of SHRM (Society for Human Resources Management). They get to attend monthly learning events and network with other professionals who they can learn from.

Sending your team out into the real world is one of the simplest ways to bolster their learning and engagement. This type of involvement outside of the office also helps to build morale among team members. When your employees are in a new setting where they don't know as many familiar faces, they will often rely on each other more than they may in the office. This kind of team building is something that deserves attention inside and outside of the office.

Utilizing outside resources

During my interviews as I prepared to write this book, several executives mentioned that they used outside resources and classes to educate their team. Tony Perricilli from Scott + Co. in Columbia, SC shared that they partner with a national alliance group to get access to resources that aid in employee development. This helps them by not only offering industry-specific training and information they would have to pay a lot more for if they went to a training company, but it is also specific to the services their firm offers. This helps them to improve their team and their operations.

You can find external training materials in a variety of places. I know plenty of accounting firms like Scott + Co. that work with outside "alliances" or associations that offer them training resources as part of their partnership. This can allow you to get extremely specific to your industry. There are also countless consultants and experts in every field who have made training materials that are specific to your industry.

When we opened a staffing division, we found a company that created an online learning portal specific to the staffing and recruiting industry. We were able to utilize this to have full, professional training courses for our team with no effort on our part. We could then cater the goals and learning objectives to our environment.

A simple Google search will help you unearth plenty of training opportunities for your team from outside companies. Make sure you understand the types of learners on your team and remember that you must hit all three learning styles (visual, audio, and kinesthetic) for the training to be a success. You should also look for training courses or opportunities that have some form of a follow-up mechanism involved (survey or testing later) so you can ensure the training stuck.

Colleges or Universities

Whether it be for one class, a certificate, or an advanced degree, there is one place that people can sometimes overlook when it comes to making their people better: higher education institutions. Sending someone to the local university or technical school can help them to not only improve their skills in the most controlled environment you can find (they will do the testing for you!), but also show your employees how committed you are to their success.

Isn't that super expensive?

Yes, it is not the cheapest option, but there are a few things to consider. Technical or community college will often offer courses or certificates for skills that your teammates might need. That includes everything from Excel and accounting to human resources.

You can offer a tuition reimbursement program to help offset the cost of your teammate's development. While this is a big investment, you can protect that investment by adding a clause into your reimbursement program that requires an employee to stay for a certain amount of time after completing the course, or they will have to return the money when they leave.

Here is a sample policy:

Employees are encouraged to take educational and training courses to improve their skills. To be eligible for education reimbursement, an employee must be full-time, have completed a year of service, and be on the payroll when the course is completed.

The Company will reimburse up to $XXXX of approved educational expenses in a year. No reimbursements for courses taken from an accredited educational institution will be made for grades lower than a C. Employees may not take courses pass/fail, unless no other grading option is available; in that case, the employee must pass in order to be reimbursed.

To receive education reimbursement, employees must follow these steps:

- *Provide their manager with information about the course for which they would like to receive reimbursement.*

- *Complete the pre-approval section of the tuition reimbursement form and provide all necessary signatures prior to enrolling.*

- *If approved, bring the form to Human Resources. A copy will be put in the employee's file and the employee will maintain the original until they have completed the course.*

- *Enroll in and attend the course.*

- *Upon completion of the course, resubmit the original education reimbursement form with the reimbursement section filled out and signed, and provide receipt(s) and evidence of a passing grade or certification.*

Additional questions should be directed to Human Resources.

SCHEDULING TRAINING

There are a few different ways to think about scheduling training. First, you need to have a process for training new employees and a continuing education path for your teammates. You then need an ongoing training program to help keep key competencies top of mind and to make your employees better. These training programs are also geared toward helping your team learn any new practices or systems within the organization.

Now, I know what you may be thinking: "How am I supposed to schedule time for training with everything else we have going on?" Well, let's first wrap our brains around the idea that training is not a loss for your business. Although time is limited during the workday for any business, the potential gains from having a training program in place far outweigh the potential losses. As I've mentioned throughout this chapter, it's all about dedicating the time during the creation of the training program to ensure needs are met and learning remains a constant.

Create a weekly, biweekly or monthly hourly goal for your employees regarding training hours completed. The training hours can be measured using an existing employee portal or other software. By creating a goal for your employees to reach, you set the expectation that continued training is a vital part of employment at your company.

At ERG Payroll & HR, it is required that you spend at least one hour a week in training. We measure this and hold people accountable to find the opportunity if we don't present it to them. By now, you have mostly all heard the story about the CEO and CFO talking about investing in training their team. The CFO asks, "What happens if we invest all this money in training our team and they leave?" to which the CEO responds, "What happens if we don't, and they stay?"

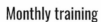

Monthly training

You should have some form of monthly training on the calendar that benefits a large portion of employees. This can be something more general that most employees can use (skills like communication, organization, time management, anti-harassment). This training is best if you can make it as close to "all hands on deck" as possible.

You should also have one team specific monthly training. This can include more specific skills and competencies that are team based, like the sales process, customer service, accounting practices, etc.

By simply putting two standing pieces of training on the calendar per month, you have ensured that your team will get a minimum of 24 hours per year in continuing education.

The execution of these training programs can be determined by using the gap analysis from above combined with the different methods of training. Plot this out at least a quarter in advance and get it on your team's calendars. Make sure everyone knows these meetings are mandatory.

BRANDING

It helps to brand your training and put it on the same schedule every time. We have branded our weekly training as "Rock Monday." Our goals are called Rocks and we do train every Monday that is in line with how we will accomplish our goals for the quarter. For example: Our current Rock is to help every one of our HR outsourcing clients to extend their onboarding program beyond new hire paperwork. We have three specific things we want to implement with each of them: a pre-hire checklist, a 30-day training plan, and a new hire scavenger hunt. That allows us to spend our time on Mondays doing training that is relevant to those goals combined with some of the other skills we recognize that are needed. We are constantly doing customer service training or case studies from companies, like the Ritz Carlton, so we can keep the importance and skills top of mind.

Employee's ownership of the learning plan

If you are just flat out opposed to doing team training because you cannot find training that is applicable to a broad enough group of your teammates, you can put your teammates in charge of their learning plans. I think one of the best examples I have found on this is from Tom Pietras at Bauknight, Pietras, and Stormer (BPS). At BPS, they have the advantage of forced learning. What do I mean by that? CPAs in South Carolina are required to complete 40 hours per year of continuing education. This is an extraordinary amount when you consider that attorneys in South Carolina are only required to complete 14 hours.

As you would expect from a company that is known for being one of the "Best Places to Work" year in and year out, they put their own spin on how employee's education is handled. They allow the employee to create their own learning plan for the year. The employee is responsible for choosing their Continuing Education Units (CEU's). This not only engages them in the process of learning but allows them to learn more about things that are interesting to them and specific to their role in the company. There is a small amount of core CEU's that the entire team participates in, but other than that, the employees are free to create their own learning plan and review it with their leader to ensure it is within budget and focused on things that can benefit the employee and company. Tom also mentioned that this process takes away complaints about "crappy training."

Mentor programs

Adding a mentor program is one of the most valuable things you can do. Giving your employees a mentor other than the person who can decide their employment fate is unbelievably valuable in the lifecycle of an employee. Think about it. Can I ever get comfortable asking my boss the dumb questions I have if I know it is going to affect their opinion of me and therefore my ability to rise within the organization? We need someone who we can talk to and ask questions.

The biggest mistake I see people make when rolling out a mentor program is not putting any criteria around it. A mentor program is like everything else—it will not work if it is not managed properly.

 A mentor program is like everything else—it will not work if it is not managed properly.

Here are a few quick tips on how to roll out a mentor program.

Train the mentors on how to coach properly.

Go to the coaching section of this book and share it with your mentors. Make sure they know how to have a valuable coaching conversation with a teammate and ask better questions. Mentors are like many leaders in that the first thing they think to do is give answers instead of asking questions. Start by asking. Allow the teammate to find their own answers.

Set the proper expectations with both the mentor and mentee so they can each get as much out of the relationship as possible.

This is a valuable way to train future leaders and aid in the development of new hires. Make sure both understand their roles in this relationship.

Once you have come to an agreement on roles and expectations, it is time for a mentee to set some goals and to develop an action plan for achieving them. Goals should be both a stretch, something inspiring to work toward that may require new skills, or the use of different "intellectual muscles," but also focused enough that the mentee can achieve them.

Goals should follow the S.M.A.R.T. goal methodology. S.M.A.R.T. goals were first introduced by George T. Doran in the November 1981 issue of AMA Forum[8]. I am not going to get into the specifics of S.M.A.R.T. goals here because they have been around so long, but if you are not familiar, the example stands for Specific, Measurable, Achievable, Realistic, and Timely. You can go to ergpayroll.com and search S.M.A.R.T. in our resources section to find plenty of resources.

Goals may also change over time. For some, setting goals will help to set the tone for the relationship. For others, time spent relationship-building will help to facilitate the process of setting goals.

Let's look at an example goal: Develop a book of 15 new clients by the end of my first year at "company."

Now, a mentee can write out an action plan to achieve that goal, including action steps. A sample action plan is included below.

Mentoring Action Plan

Goal: Develop a book of 15 new clients by the end of my first year at "company."

Action Steps

1. Identify and meet with 2-3 team members to learn how they landed their first accounts.

2. Identify and meet with 2-3 new prospects per week.

3. Identify and join at least 1 networking group outside of the office.

Investing in your people is the best way for an organization to gain a competitive advantage in business. Like any investment, if you are not disciplined in your research and execution, you can lose more than you win. Take the time to work through these steps thoroughly and maximize your return. Past performance is

---

[8]   *https://community.mis.temple.edu/mis0855002fall2015/files/2015/10/ S.M.A.R.T-Way-Management-Review.pdf*

no indication of future results. Luckily, you have control over the outcome of this stock's performance.

During Chapter 7, we dove into creating a training program for your team and how to execute it successfully. Let's recap some of the chapter's biggest takeaways.

- A detailed training program for each member of your team is vital to their development as an employee of your company. Training must be developed in a way that serves the needs of all types of learners, including visual, audio, and kinesthetic.

- Ask your team questions to determine their needs or areas of improvement that could be positively impacted by an updated training program.

- When it comes to executing your training program, ensure your team has the resources and support they need to make it a consistent occurrence, not a one-time event.

- Utilize internal and external resources to create an environment where you team looks forward to training.

CHAPTER 8:

PERFORMANCE MANAGEMENT

"Treat employees like they make a difference, and they will."
— **Jim Goodnight, CEO, SAS**

PERFORMANCE MANAGEMENT PROCESS

While there are many elements to building a culture of great-ness, none of them matter if your people are not performing. If you are doing everything you can to attract the best people in the world and then not managing that asset effectively, you will see poor performance.

We have reviewed and implemented hundreds of different per-formance management programs and found the most critical el-ements of driving high performance. The most critical factors are the consistency of the program, the simplicity of the program, and the "buy-in" from the leadership team. The performance re-view process has tremendous value to a small business. This is an opportunity to provide recognition, work on a development plan, and set goals with your team members.

Let's face it, performance reviews can be painful, awkward conversations. Plus, it can be hard to measure if the review really has an impact on overall productivity. To add to the challenge, at the end of the conversation, your team member probably wants a raise!

The good news is that your employees want performance re-views for more than just raises. They crave and need the feedback that a good performance management system will give them. By implementing and maintaining the simple process outlined be-low, you can make your team more productive and engaged. We are going to walk through a simple process for rolling out performance reviews that you can have done and ready to execute in a couple of hours.

How can I find time to do performance reviews and run my business?

This is the biggest objection we get. "We don't have time" and "Things are so crazy." As I mentioned in Chapter 7 regarding the execution of the training program, performance reviews are also not going to be a loss for your business. By establishing and maintaining a schedule for performance reviews, you set the precedent for your employees and yourself. Make the time for your employees to have performance reviews, since they are, in fact, your number one asset and they deserve to be treated like they are.

Performance management should not be viewed as optional. Employees crave it—and you need it to improve the performance of your company. Additionally, the insight you get from the process is paramount to running your business.

FIVE STEPS TO CREATING A SIMPLE PERFORMANCE MANAGEMENT SYSTEM

1. Create a Scorecard for the Role

A Scorecard helps you to maintain consistency throughout your performance evaluation process. Once you have completed a Scorecard, it can be used in all phases of the employment relationship and adjusted based on the expectations for the person in the role. You can weave it into the interviewing, hiring, training, and performance management process to help you grade candidates (and teammates) easier. This creates consistency throughout the hiring and performance management process.

A Scorecard includes a "Mission" and desired outcomes for the role. A Scorecard is different than the traditional job description in that it gives us a way to measure effectiveness instead of just checking boxes. What does a job description tell you? Vague descriptions of what needs to be done. As a matter of fact, many people have this mindset that the vaguer, the better. That way they can ask the person to do a bunch of other things. For example, A job description might say, "Provide reports to the management team" whereas a Scorecard might say "Provide the ABC, XYZ, and CBA report to all members of the executive committee prior to the board meeting on the second Tuesday of each month." Now we can measure the effectiveness of this person's ability.

Below is an example of a Scorecard you can use for your roles:

ROLE SCORECARD

Role: Customer Support Manager

Teammate: Johnny Support   **Supervisor:** Jimmy Support II

Date:11/26/2015

MISSION: The mission for this role is to create a high-end experience for our clients through world-class implementation and support.

OUTCOMES

	OUTCOMES	RATING and COMMENTS 1 - Poor 2 - Below Average 3 - Average 4 - Above Average 5 - Excellent
1	**IMPLEMENTATION:** Successfully implement 26 new clients while establishing and following SOP's that contribute to the long-term retention of clients. 100 percent data accuracy during setup of accounts prior to first processing.	4. Completed 24 new implementations with an accuracy rate of 90 percent. We had several implementation issues that need to be fixed.
2	**CLIENT SATISFACTION:** Achieve 90 percent customer satisfaction by selling appropriately scoped software, and by providing excellent training and support.	5. Achieved 92 percent NPS score amongst clients. This was an increase of 2 percent over last year.
3	**MARGIN:** Increase gross margin from 18 percent to 25 percent through cost control, by automating processes, vendor consolidation, and coordinating team prioritization.	4. Johnny increased margins to 21 percent. He did a good job of automating but lacked in vendor consolidation.
4	**CLIENT RETENTION:** Build a client touch model that improves response time to under one hour and includes one proactive touch per client, per month. Execute, track, and report on the results.	4. Johnny has improved the retention model significantly and executed on each of these initiatives.
5	**STRATEGY:** Contribute to the new 2017 strategic plan; create the support part of the plan, which syncs with marketing and finance, by 12/31/2016.	3.

CORE COMPETENCIES

What are the competencies that are most important to being successful in this role and how does the candidate/ teammate rank in each?

Competency	Grade (1–5)
Quality: The extent to which an employee's work is accurate, thorough and neat.	
Productivity: The extent to which an employee produces a significant volume of work efficiently in a specified period of time.	
Attendance and Punctuality: The extent to which an employee adheres to established work schedules and is timely for meetings or other scheduled visits or appointments with clients, employees and/or applicants.	
Job Knowledge: The extent to which an employee possesses the practical/ technical knowledge required on the job.	
Training Effectiveness: The extent to which an employee is able to grasp new ideas, methods or concepts, the speed of learning and retention.	
Communication: The extent to which an employee demonstrates written and verbal communication skills.	
Initiative: The extent to which an employee seeks out new assignments and assumes additional duties when necessary.	

Competency	Grade (1-5)
Interpersonal Relationships: The extent to which an employee is willing and demonstrates the ability to cooperate, work, and communicate with coworkers and supervisors.	
Service Relationships: The extent to which an employee is willing and demonstrates the ability to cooperate, work and communicate with clients, applicants, and employees, and successfully builds rapport with them.	
Dependability: Reliability in following through on assignments and instructions.	
Judgment: The extent to which an employee demonstrates proper judgment and decision-making skills when necessary.	

You can see in the above example that I was able to boil the role down into the five most important outcomes that align with our company goals. This helps me as a leader to make sure that all my teammates are in line with company goals. It also helps me to easily review the company goals with the teammate at each review and keep them top of mind.

In the competencies section, I can review the teammate against the most important competencies. How can we evaluate what is most important? Go back to the training survey. Your team has already told you if you followed through with that exercise. Now you can pare this list down so that we do not have a bunch of competencies on here that are not important to the mission.

The thing I see people do wrong all the time on these Scorecards is they still want to keep them vague. They want to put "Improve client satisfaction" instead of "Achieve 90 percent customer satisfaction by selling appropriately-scoped software, and by providing excellent training and support." You have to hold your team accountable and lead by example when it comes to the performance management process. This includes maintaining consistency with your reviews of your leadership team and making sure that you allow your team to assess you. The feedback you can get from performing a self-assessment and allowing your team to assess your performance is invaluable. The key here (like everything else) is to *execute* when you recognize things that need to change.

2. Review the Scorecard and Performance Action Plan with Teammate

Once you complete the Scorecard for the role, you have done your part. Now it is time to put action into the teammate's hands. Start this process by reviewing the Scorecard, getting their buy off on it, and introducing them to the Performance Action Plan. This plan will be their way of identifying how they are going to achieve these goals. The other point of this is to review our Core Values with the teammate. You will see the first question is "What do we believe in?" This is a little bit of a test to make sure your teammates are on the same page with everything we have talked about in this book. Your Core Values should run through everything you do, most importantly the expectations we have related to performance.

The question "How do we do it here?" is a good way to gauge understanding of if your employees understand your competitive advantage in the marketplace. I am often surprised to see how many leaders cannot properly articulate this. If your team cannot properly articulate "why" you are better than the competition, you probably never will be.

Next, you want to have them complete three goals for the next 12 months. They will have the ability to "cheat" by having these align with their Scorecard. Get them to think hard about these goals by asking, "If these were the only things I accomplished in the next 12 months, the year would be a success." You will have to push on some people to get them in the right line of thinking, especially the first few times through. Then you want to back that down into the next 90 days. How will you get closer to those three goals in the next 90 days? Break it down into chunks. We follow that up with a simple *Stop, Start, Continue.*

Stop—What am I doing right now that I need to stop? What are the things that are not moving me toward my goals or preventing my success? What are my bad habits?

Examples often include not prioritizing my day, spending too much time dealing with X task, etc.

Start—What are the things I am not doing that I need to start? Examples include planning my day before I leave the day before, turning off all distractions when I am working on a project, etc.

Continue—What am I doing that is really working that I need to continue? Examples include showing up on time, having daily stand up meetings with the support team, completing all of my TPS reports on time, etc.

See the below template. You can also find this at ergpayroll. com/book

Performance Action Plan

Name:
Date:

What do we believe in?
What are the core values of our company?

_____

_____

How do we do it here?
How do we execute better than our competition?

_____

_____

Three Goals for the Next 12 Months
If these were the only things I accomplished in the next 12 months, the year would be a success.

_____

_____

Three Goals for the Next 90 Days
Accomplishing these three goals in the next 90 days will help me achieve my goals for the year.

_____

_____

STOP	START	CONTINUE
What am I doing right now that I need to stop?	What should I start doing to be more successful?	What am I doing that is really working that I need to continue?

3. Teammate Completes Action Plan

This is the easy part (for you). Allow your team member one week to complete the Performance Action Plan and schedule a follow-up date to review. Remind them that the Performance Action Plan is not "set in stone" and you will review the content and goals to adjust for success. Provide the teammate with the S.M.A.R.T. goal setting guide and their Scorecard to ensure alignment. You can find templates for both at ergpayroll.com/book.

4. Review the Action Plan with the Teammate

During this meeting, you can tweak the goals to ensure they are S.M.A.R.T. and align with the Scorecard. Make sure you understand *WHY* each goal is important to the team member and they understand the mission of the organization. Ask a lot of questions and do not lead the team member—let them find their own answers.

I cannot stress enough that you are prepared and able to turn their goals into S.M.A.R.T. goals. Eight times out of ten, people will not get this on the first try. They will come to you with some vague goals and not understand what you are going for. That is ok. Help them get on the right track. That is your job as a leader.

5. Set Dates for Quarterly (and Monthly) Reviews

Set dates with the teammate for the quarterly performance review. Set a reminder to provide the team member with the Self-Assessment one week prior. Review the Performance Action Plan monthly with the employee to track goal progress. You can add and take away goals as they are accomplished. This meeting can be anywhere from 20 minutes to an hour. Take this time to ask a lot of questions.

You should complete an assessment and the teammate should complete one, too. The assessment should contain questions related to three areas:

- Scorecard/Goals
- Performance of Competencies
- Representation of Core Values

Here is an example of an assessment that you would complete. The employee version is nearly identical. You can find this at ergpayroll.com/book:

Quarterly Employee Assessment

If a teammate has been employed by the company less than a year, substitute references to "since the last performance appraisal" with "since you were hired" and answer the questions accordingly. Supervisors: Attach completed self-assessments to the Employee's Performance Appraisal and attach to the employee's online file.

Leader Name: _____

Teammate Name:_____

List the teammate's most significant accomplishments or contributions since last year. How do these achievements align with the company goals?
Comments:
Since the last appraisal period, has the teammate successfully performed any new tasks or additional duties outside the scope of their regular responsibilities? If so, please specify.
Comments:
What activities has teammate initiated, or actively participated in, to encourage camaraderie and teamwork within your group and/or office? What was the result?
Comments:
To which of the following factors would you attribute their professional development since last year: offsite seminars/classes (specify if self-directed or required by supervisor), onsite training, peer training, management coaching or mentoring, on-the-job experience, better exposure to challenging projects, or other—please describe.
Comments:
Describe areas you feel require improvement in terms of their professional capabilities. List the steps they plan to take and/or the resources they need to accomplish this.

Comments:

Studies have shown that high customer satisfaction and employee satisfaction are linked. What are their ideas for improving the company's client and/or employee satisfaction and retention?
Comments:

State two goals you have for this teammate for the coming year and indicate how you plan to help them accomplish the goals.
Comments:

Core Values
Evaluate the teammate on all of ERG Payroll & HR's Core Values. How well does he/she represent each of these on a scale of 1 to 5 and what can you do to help them improve?

	(1 = Poor - 5 = Awesome)
Servant Leadership	
Work Hard on the Right Things	
Fanatical Attention to Detail	
Grow or Die	
Be Flexible	
Competency	Rating (1-5) with Notes

Additional Notes:

Competency	Rating (1–5) with Notes
Quality: The extent to which an employee's work is accurate, thorough and neat.	
Productivity: The extent to which an employee produces a significant volume of work efficiently in a specified period of time.	
Attendance and Punctuality: The extent to which an employee adheres to established work schedules and is timely for meetings or other scheduled visits or appointments with clients, employees and/or applicants.	
Job Knowledge: The extent to which an employee possesses the practical/technical knowledge required on the job.	
Training Effectiveness: The extent to which an employee is able to grasp new ideas, methods or concepts, the speed of learning and retention.	
Communication: The extent to which an employee demonstrates written and verbal communication skills.	
Initiative: The extent to which an employee seeks out new assignments and assumes additional duties when necessary.	
Interpersonal Relationships: The extent to which an employee is willing and demonstrates the ability to cooperate, work, and communicate with coworkers and supervisors.	

Competency	Rating (1–5) with Notes
Service Relationships: The extent to which an employee is willing and demonstrates the ability to cooperate, work and communicate with clients, applicants, and employees, and successfully builds rapport with them.	
Dependability: Reliability in following through on assignments and instructions.	
Judgment: The extent to which an employee demonstrates proper judgment and decision-making skills when necessary.	

Your assessment and the self-assessment should be nearly identical. This is where the magic happens. This is how you know if the system is working. How close are your responses? If the employee thinks they are a 5 at representing several of your Core Values and you think they are a two, it is time to talk.

BONUS

The way that we ensure we are always on the same page is with monthly "Plan and Review" meetings. These meetings are an opportunity to take a step back and talk about the teammate's career, their goals, what is going well, and anything they may need to continue performing at their job. We try not to talk about specific projects or updates unless they want to. This is their time. You are just there to ask questions. You can have this short meeting every month (30 minutes) and then do the assessments on the quarters. This keeps it simple.

Make sure you have a good system for keeping up with the notes. We are an HR technology company, so obviously we use our HR system (you can find out more at ergpayroll.com), but you need to document them in some way. There is nothing more powerful (and useful) than being able to reference notes from a year ago when having the monthly one-on-one meeting. I have seen people's answer of "where do you see yourself in two years" change drastically in one year's time. It is important you ask. I have also asked someone to rate their happiness on a scale of 1-10 and they said a 5! They were at a 9 the last time I asked. I found out that she was doing a lot of work she did not want to be doing. This was bumming her out. We put a plan in place to spread the work around and help her out. Like I said, you will never know unless you ask!

Use this template to guide the conversation. Pick two to three of these questions each month and shut your mouth. Once again, you can find this at ergpayroll.com/book.

MONTHLY 1:1 MEETING

Select a few questions each month to get a pulse on your team-mate's engagement level, identify ways you can help them to get better at their job, and increase productivity.

<u>Let them do most of the talking.</u>

What WINS have you had since our last conversation?

What can we do to help make you more effective at your job?

Is there anything you are not doing today that you would like to be doing?

What is one area of personal growth that you would like to improve on?

What have you done to move closer to achieving your goals (have quarterly and annual goals available)?

How do you monitor that?

_____

What would you like to be doing in two years?

_____

What part of the job do you like best?

_____

What is your least favorite part of the job?

_____

How would you rate your happiness in your current role on a scale of 1-10? What would improve that rating?

_____

What are some things you want to improve on?

_____

What do you think we could do to improve how we serve our customers?

_____

How can we make this a better place to work?

_____

Can you provide me with some feedback on how I can be a better leader?

_____

Takeaways from the meeting:

_____

_____

_____

Action Items for Me:

_____

_____

_____

_____

COMMUNICATE THE PLAN TO THE TEAM

When you are preparing to roll this process out, it is important to outline the new performance process to your team. This will not only help them to understand what to expect, but it will help you to hold you accountable to executing on the plan consistently.

Nothing turns an employee off more than getting a review one year and not the next. You can kill engagement and productivity by letting your process slip. After you communicate clear expectations to the team, you need to hold yourself and the management team accountable to following through.

Make sure that you are using your process of choice to ensure this gets done every time it is scheduled. It starts with a simple calendar reminder and can be something as complex as a full-blown performance management system.

Now, you are prepared to update or start your performance management program. Don't miss out on an opportunity to identify issues with an employee before a major problem develops. You can increase retention, improve employee development, and get more out of your team by taking the time to analyze what they are doing and how they can improve. Remember, your team wants the feedback!

CHAPTER 8 TAKEAWAYS

Before we move on to Chapter 9, let's reflect on what we learned about performance reviews.

- Employees crave performance reviews. As your company's biggest asset, they deserve to have regular reviews that keep them engaged.
- Performance reviews are not a loss for your company. Make the time for your employees.
- The Performance Action Plan keeps you and your team accountable when it comes to goal setting.

CHAPTER 9:

EMPLOYEE RECOGNITION

"95% of my assets drive out the gate every evening.
It is my job to maintain a work environment that keeps those people
coming back every day."
— **Jim Goodnight, CEO, SAS**

We've all had the conversation. *"Got a minute."* One of your valued teammates sits you down to tell you they are leaving.

"It's not you, it's me."

Ugh. All that knowledge, experience, time, and energy walking out the door.

Employee turnover can kill a small business. It costs a lot of money, puts tremendous strain on the existing staff, and can be demoralizing.

HOW DO YOU PREVENT EMPLOYEE TURNOVER?

Employees not only want good pay and benefits, but they also want to be treated well and feel appreciated for their efforts.

To show appreciation, many employers conduct ongoing recognition programs designed to thank employees for a variety of achievements. In a recent survey by SHRM and the recognition consulting firm Globoforce, 80 percent of organizations reported having an employee recognition program.[9]

Organizations adopt employee recognition programs to raise employee morale; attract and retain key employees; elevate productivity; increase competitiveness, revenues, and profitability;

---

[9]   *http://go.globoforce.com/rs/862-JIQ-698/images/*
SHRM2017_GloboforceEmployeeRecognitionReportFinal.pdf?_
ga=2.163866175.1806273419.1562496873-1788112948.1562496873

improve quality, safety, and customer service; and reduce employee stress, absenteeism, and turnover.

Rewards range from simple spoken or written thank-you notes and "spot" bonuses of gift cards to catalog merchandise and even vacation packages.

There are countless ways to reward employees that fit every budget. However, it is important to give some thought on how you structure your program in order to realize those returns on productivity and employee engagement.

Most companies start a program, and it fizzles out over time, or they try to put too much in place and it becomes an administrative hassle and time-consuming nightmare.

To put together an effective employee recognition program, focus on these three key questions:

1. What events and behaviors do you want to recognize?
2. How much time/resources do you have to dedicate to the program?
3. How will you track the program?

Remember **consistency is key**. People like being rewarded, and even more importantly, like being treated fairly. If Susan hears that Bob got a birthday card and she didn't get one, Susan will feel let down.

Inconsistency will undermine the program and leave some employees feeling worse than if there was not any recognition at all. So, make sure your programs are realistic for your time and your budget.

Recognizing top performers not only rewards them, but it also encourages the same behavior in others. Recognize the actions you want to see duplicated.

RECOGNITION-WORTHY EVENTS

Performance:

- Teamwork
- Top performers
- Business wins
- Customer satisfaction or retention
- Actions and behaviors that embody the organization's core values
- Innovation
- Project completion

Milestones:

- Work anniversaries—pick significant years like 1, 3, 5, 10
- Retirements
- Employee birthdays
- Family births
- Holidays

According to the 2018 SHRM/ Globoforce Employee Recognition Survey:

"Values-based recognition programs – where employees are recognized and rewarded for behavior that exemplifies a company's core values – continue to be more highly adopted (70 percent) than recognition programs not tied to a company's core values (30 percent).*"

EMPLOYEE RECOGNITION IDEAS

Free Employee Recognition Ideas

Team Meetings: Allow five minutes for each team meeting or every other team meeting to recognize employees for their hard work. Managers can recognize their employees and even allow time for employees to recognize each other.

*Take note of who is recognized at each meeting and review periodically to make sure you are spreading the love around.

Tip: *Recognize Your Core Values and Goals: recognition is most effective when it's given in the context of a larger goal or business-results-focused activity. Random affirmations are much less meaningful than those tied to a business goal. If your goal is to drive growth, an employee who lands a big contract by putting in the extra effort and following company processes needs to know you noticed.*

Written Praise: You can do this with an email or an old-fashioned handwritten note. When you recognize an employee this way, be sure to give them specifics on their accomplishments just as you would at a team event.

Tip: *If you are a business owner or a manager, make a goal to send out a thank you note to a team member once a week, or a month, depending on the size of your team.*

Hold your managers accountable. *Have them report on who they recognize on their teams, and coach them if they don't understand the value.*

Cards for Significant Occasions: For significant occasions, such as an employee's birthday, or family member birth or death, you do not have to grab your wallet to make them feel appreciated. Get a card and collect signatures from other team members.

Cheap Employee Appreciation Ideas

Prize Tokens: When you see someone doing something nice for someone else or go the extra mile for a customer, recognize them by handing out a performance token. After they collect two or three tokens, let them pick out a "prize" like a gift card or something for their office.

On the Spot: Create an office symbol to use at meetings. "Coffee's for closers" coffee mug or the "hit it out of the park" baseball bat. Come up with something that is unique to your team.

At ERG Payroll & HR, we have a Buzz Lightyear to symbolize when someone goes "to infinity and beyond" for the team. Give it to a team member when you see them doing something recognition worthy. *You can also do this at your meeting.* Let the employee keep it on display in their office for a week or two and then give it to someone else.

Keep $5, $10 or $20 gift cards to Starbucks, Target or Amazon on-hand for recognizing actions in real time.

Organize a Company Lunch: Make sure you take the time to recognize and say a few words about the employee.

Not-So-Cheap Appreciation Ideas

Because work anniversaries are less frequent and are at the heart of recognizing employee loyalty, these should be a bit more thought out and splurge worthy.

Vacation Bonus: This is obviously one of the more expensive ways to thank employees for their service, so pick a year that is truly a milestone, such as 5 or 10. Allot a certain amount to go toward a vacation. At ERG Payroll & HR, we pay $10,000 toward a vacation anywhere in the world at your 5-year anniversary.

Present Catalog: Companies like Terry Berry provide the catalog and ordering service for your service awards. You set the price level for each anniversary and the employee will pick what they want from the catalog.

Personalized Gifts: Set monetary limits for each anniversary or choose specific items for each anniversary. Companies like Things Remembered will engrave the employee's name, the company name, and the occasion.

TRACKING YOUR EMPLOYEE RECOGNITION PROGRAM

Regardless of what you choose to recognize, make sure you are consistent, and you have the appropriate resources to track the program. This can range from a simple Excel spreadsheet, all the way to software designed for tracking employee information.

A Few Keys to Tracking the Program

Make sure more than one person has access to the information. This is where Excel lets you down. It does not track real-time edits—if you add a new hire, but do not save the latest version on the share drive, no one else has it.

There is another great free tool for this: Trello. If you have not used Trello before, this is a project management tool that has a free version, which is perfect for managing processes like a recognition program. You can set reminders, tag people, access via mobile, and more.

Some human resources software has features built in for employee recognition software. Our platform, Guhroo, has birthday and anniversary reminders along with an announcement feature for you to share information with the entire team. Combine this with the ongoing employee engagement surveys and you will have a full arsenal of tools to engage your team.

Your employees are your most important asset, make sure you treat them as such!

How to Get Started

- Take an inventory of any current or past employee recognition programs. What worked and what did not work?
- Answer the below three questions and document what your goals are for recognizing employee performance.
    1. What events and behaviors do you want to recognize?
    2. How much time/resources do you have to dedicate to the program?
    3. How will you track the program?
- Get started! A simple thank you to teammates goes a long way. Recognize someone today.

CHAPTER 9 TAKEAWAYS

Recognizing your employees is crucial to maintaining an awesome culture. Let's recap the main points that we covered in this chapter.

- Showing appreciation for your teammates is more than just a one-time thing. Consistency is key.

- Recognize the actions of others in your company that you wish to see duplicated.

- Employee recognition does not require a large budget. It is all about providing your teammates with the recognition they deserve for being an asset to your company culture.

CHAPTER 10:

COACHING

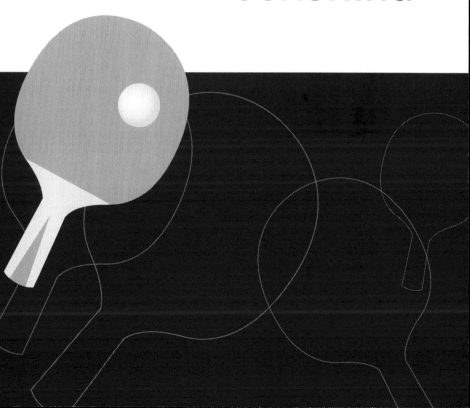

"It's what you learn after you know it all, that counts."
— **John Wooden, UCLA Basketball Coach**

"I can't figure out why this keeps happening," my client said to me. He was frustrated. Another employee left, unexpectedly to him. He sat across from me in a conference room in their office. They had an office just like those you would see in any business park in America. It was a plain two-story building with a shared entrance. There were signs on a wall for each company when you walked in. The shared conference room was right in front of you.

"Why do you think she left?" I asked him.

It is always hard to know exactly why someone leaves a company, but it is rarely ever because they are incredibly happy and just received an offer they could not refuse.

"She left for more money. We just can't compete with what these big firms offer." He took her at her word. He asked if there was anything they could do to make her stay. She said there was not. Another one bites the dust.

This is a common situation and resulting thought process from small business owners: "We are inferior to large companies and when they come calling with their big checkbooks, we are going to lose." While this thought pattern is common, it is not always the case. As a matter of fact, many employees would rather make less if they are happy and have a good leadership team than leave to make a few more dollars.

In this situation, we did an exit interview with the employee. This is a common thing for us. We set up a call with the employee either while they are in their last two weeks or just after they leave. They talk to one of our HR business partners for quite a while. These calls work well because we are an independent third party that they feel comfortable sharing the things that they want their former employer to know, but don't want to tell them directly. As a matter of fact, the calls are often so detailed that we have to water them down a little before sharing with the employer.

During my conversation with the employee who unexpectedly left, I gained insight into the real reasons why she decided to leave. She said to me, "He is just an a**hole. That is all there is to it. I can't work for him anymore. Every time I walk in that building, I feel sick."

She was not the only one who said that during an exit interview.

The above employee left because she did not like the culture, thought the communication was poor, and always worked in fear that she would lose her job at any moment if she made even the smallest mistake. She went on to tell us story after story about situations when the business owner had cut her down in front of her team—criticized them every time they were having fun, as if it was not possible to have fun at work. She explained how it was impossible to get any work done because he was constantly changing systems and the goals for the team, all of which became blurrier over time. And, after all that, she mentioned how she was going to make a little more money at her new job.

The money was the last thing on the list of reasons why she was leaving. *It usually is.*

Was this turnover avoidable? Oh yeah. She did leave for a dollar more, but would she have stayed if she had not felt that way in her work environment?

So, the question begs, what can you do to prevent similar circumstances from happening at your company? First, don't be an a**hole. While that might sound terse, I am serious. It is amazing how often small business owners lack empathy and think that all their employees should be incredibly grateful for their jobs and live to serve every whim of the owner—and the business—with no regard for their own wellbeing.

How does this look in the day to day? In addition to the practices, we have covered so far, feedback and coaching are foundational to the success of your team and organization. Feedback and coaching (with the wrong intent) can be extremely dangerous. The client mentioned above thought he was coaching his teammates toward success. He had a different style of coaching (a bad one) and was only worried about one thing: the bottom line.

If you take the time to do all of the things that we mentioned in this book well, the bottom line will take care of itself.

There is a reason that employees are asked on the "Best Places to Work" survey about the amount of feedback they receive:

 People crave, want, and need feedback.

We need it. It is like water to a plant. We need to know what we are doing well or wrong so we can do more of the good and improve on the bad. It is really that simple. If someone does not realize that what they are doing is wrong, how can they improve? Not to mention, when they encounter a tough situation, they will face again, they need to know the best way to handle it.

Let's start by answering one question: *Where does coaching fit into giving employee feedback?*

WHAT IS EMPLOYEE COACHING?

"A style of management primarily characterized by asking employees questions in order to help them fulfill their immediate responsibilities more effectively and advance their development as professionals over time."—*Harvard Business Review* "Guide to Coaching Employees"

Employee coaching allows you to not only give feedback in a productive way, but it also allows employees to find their own answers and be empowered in the process. This process creates a higher level of learning and aptitude amongst your team.

WHAT IS YOUR DEFINITION OF EMPLOYEE COACHING?

I ask this question to executives whenever we are doing one-on-one training for employee coaching. Since they know they are being led to water a little bit, they will often give answers that are like the *Harvard Business Review* definition above. While they all answer very similarly about what it should be and how it looks when done effectively, most leaders will admit to not executing now.

WHY IS IT SO HARD TO COACH PROPERLY?

Simply put, it's not. It can just be uncomfortable. The reality is that your success will be defined by the number of uncomfortable conversations you are willing to have. If you are not willing to address employee actions in real time, then they will not be able to learn and get better. Ultimately, you will be the one to suffer, not them. You can avoid some of this discomfort by setting proper expectations during the interview process and throughout the first 90 days. By letting someone know your culture is about high-velocity feedback, you can prepare them for the coaching they are about to receive. By coaching them early and often, you can make these conversations more comfortable.

We also often think of coaching as to how we see coaches in sports. They have a game plan, they teach it to their team, and then they yell and scream at teammates during the game if an assignment is missed. While this might seem like a simpler way to handle things (come on, we all want to yell at people from time to time), it is the worst way to handle things.

People do not need to be yelled at—they need to learn from doing. They need to know when they missed an assignment in real time, but they also need to do it in a way that allows them to think and come to their own conclusions.

Have you ever left a meeting with your boss and your brain just hurt? I remember one of my old bosses—every time we would sit down, he would ask me questions that made me think. We had a weekly conversation where he would sit there on the other side of his big, L-shaped desk with his neatly arranged piles and just ask me questions. One question after another. It was painful at the moment.

I never felt like I had the right answer. I was pulling from deep inside myself (I know we did a training on this at some point!). I had been told all of the information as part of my training that all employees go through—which was more like drinking from a fire-hose—but I had not truly learned the information. It took some bad repetitions and some reflection before I really "got it."

The questions he asked were very simply his way of allowing me to find the answers he knew I had. He saw that I had practiced the plays, but just did not execute them at game time. He knew that I could be a star performer and he was not going to let me get away with just being "good enough."

 This is important. Your role as the coach can define someone's career.

WHO NEEDS COACHING?

The short answer is everyone. This includes you. There has never been an Olympic athlete without a coach. There will never be a championship team without a coach. High performance occurs under the watch of a skilled coach. Guess what those coaches also need? Coaching! They can't be the best coaches in the world without being coached themselves. They also benefit immensely from coaching their team. There is nothing more rewarding than watching someone spread their wings and fly after trying so hard to succeed, and you were there to guide them down the right path. Coaching is valuable to everyone involved.

There are several forms of value that come out of coaching. The first is probably the most obvious: employee development. When you have better, more frequent conversations with employees that are aimed at helping them improve and discover their own answers, you will see their productivity increase, their morale increases, and they will stay in their jobs longer. People want to be good at what they do.

This reminds me of a conversation I had with a client about two years ago. It was the kind of conversation I had many times before. "Matt, we need to fire Susie, what do we need to do to make this happen?"

"Great, we are happy to help. Didn't Susie just start two weeks ago? What happened?" I asked.

"She's just not a fit. She doesn't get it. Things aren't getting done the way we need them to be." He told me. He was convinced that this new teammate was not going to be good after two weeks.

"Have you talked to her about it?" I asked.

"Yeah, I think someone has. The other girls tell her what she should be doing but she just doesn't get it. She has been doing the same things wrong over and over."

"Are you sure this has been addressed? Have you talked to her yourself?" I asked.

"No. I guess I am not sure, and I have not talked to her."

No one should ever be surprised when they are fired. You should have warned them about their behavior and given them the opportunity to improve or they should have done something so crazy that they knew they were going to get fired for it.

In this circumstance, we had several issues. She was not properly trained (hard to do the job right when there is no formal training) and then the leader refused to coach her and help her improve. We see this even more in small businesses where the leaders want to delegate everything and focus on growing the business. They often forget that you cannot delegate leadership!

I then talked with the client again and advised him to sit down with her and ask what she thought about the particular things he believed she was doing wrong. The biggest thing I wanted him to remember was to have an open mind. It would certainly be a lot cheaper and easier to help raise the performance level of this employee than to start the hiring process over again. He had this job open for months before hiring her.

During the conversation, she explained what she was thinking and how she was told to do things. In one case, the way she was doing it was better than what they were currently doing. She had brought the practice from her old company. He started to understand that she was confused a lot because of the minimal training. She was trying her best to do the job with minimal support. He took the opportunity to walk her through some of the best practices and what they expected. He also opened the lines of communication between the two of them while also showing her how to get information when he was busy. She still works there today. She is a core member of the team and does a wonderful job.

Employee coaching will result in increased productivity and improved culture while also helping you create a succession plan. Not sure what I mean by a succession plan? Succession planning at its core is training your leadership replacement for the future. You cannot always plan when someone on your leadership team will retire. But you can plan ahead and make sure someone else on your team is prepared to take their role. This reiterates the importance of consistent training. You can't expect someone on your team to fill another's shoes if they haven't been properly trained throughout their career at your organization.

WHAT COACHING IS NOT

Coaching vs. Progressive Discipline

It is useful to contrast a coaching approach to progressive discipline, which many workplaces utilize. Unlike progressive discipline, a coaching approach is not a "top-down "approach. Progressive discipline typically follows the steps of verbal counseling, written warnings, possible other consequences, final warning and then termination if the behavior does not improve. While progressive discipline helps protect the employer from liability resulting from discrimination charges and lawsuits, it often fails to bring about the kind of behavioral change that transforms employees into fully functioning, committed team members.

What are three situations where coaching employees can have a high impact?

1. **Training**—Helping employees learn by debriefing situations and asking lots of questions will allow you to touch all styles or learners and meet them where they learn best.

2. **Poor Performer**—Someone who is having trouble might not be lost. They may just be unclear on expectations or how to perform their job responsibilities. Coaching can help you to identify if they are fit to be a long-term teammate or need to be coached out.

3. **Star Performer (Growth mindset)**—Helping your star performers grow will benefit everyone. These are the people you need to be sure you are spending time coaching. Too often we spend all of our time providing feedback and coaching to our underperformers when there could be a much higher return on investment coaching our star performers.

COACHING REQUIRES A GROWTH MINDSET

In the wonderful book "Mindset" by Carol Dweck, she shares the differences between a fixed and a growth mindset. We have all had a fixed mindset in the workplace before. You assign a task to a teammate, they don't do it as you expected, so you think they are not capable of performing that function and you don't let them do it again.

With a growth mindset, we would realize that maybe the teammate did not have enough training and will get better at it with more repetitions. We understand that just because a child falls over and over when attempting to walk, does not mean they will never walk. We invest time in making that person better and improving the process, so it is easier for new teammates to learn. A fixed mindset will close off walls inside your business and will stop you from creating the type of culture that people want to be a part of.

WHAT ARE THE DIFFERENCES BETWEEN A FIXED AND GROWTH MINDSET?

Fixed	Growth
Intelligence is static	Intelligence can be developed
Avoids challenge	Embraces challenge
Gives up easily when faced with obstacles	Persistence to overcome obstacles
Sees little or no value in effort	Effort = path to success
Ignores criticism	Learns from criticism
Feels threatened by the success of others	Learns from the success of others

These mindsets lead to radically different attitudes for employees. The employee with a fixed mindset becomes stagnant and tends to plateau short of their true potential. On the other hand, the growth mindset creates a greater sense of free will for an employee, ultimately leading them to seemingly limitless potential.

STEPS TO IMPROVE EMPLOYEE PERFORMANCE THROUGH COACHING

Let's take a look at a simple framework you can use every day to coach your teammates and develop them. Below is an outline of the R.E.A.C.T. model of employee coaching that I created to help our clients to better recognize and address coaching situations in real time.

Recognize

Everyone can benefit from coaching as both employees and supervisors can fall into a routine. Coaching is a good reminder and an opportunity for employee and supervisor to come up with ideas for improvement (growth mindset).

Identify opportunities to coach as they happen during the workday. Just finished a meeting that was led by a teammate and recognized opportunities for improvement? Stop and ask them questions. Help them learn how to execute better next time. Many leaders I work with have to start by making the time. You should start with frequent, short conversations. Find two to three people on your team and dedicate ten minutes per week to coaching them. You should put this on your calendar or to-do list to help you remember.

Finding the time to coach your team will make them more autonomous, engaged, and productive.

Expectations

Providing proper expectations from the time you interview someone and consistently throughout your employment relationship will make the impact of your coaching much more powerful. Coaching is a collaborative process. Make sure that employees know you will be looking for ways to help them grow and the expectation is that they have goals for their career.

What if you did not set these expectations initially and have not been coaching your team up until now? Tell them now! Moving forward, I am going to do a better job of providing you with feedback and coaching so that you can continue to grow in your career and get better. Who doesn't want to get better?

Ask Better Questions

Instead of giving the employee the solution to a problem (*more of a "command and control" style*), you assume the employee has the wisdom within to <u>come to answers on their own</u>. They can't do this if you just hit them over the head with the answers all the time.

Sometimes you may know a possible answer, but sometimes (as is the case with employees who handle extremely specific technical information) you may not. With a coaching approach, you ask instead of advice as much as possible. <u>If you provide an answer, you limit the possible outcomes</u>. We will review some questions you can ask shortly.

Create a Feedback Loop

Coaching works best when <u>employees assume ownership</u> over their own professional development and improvement. It is a *collaborative* approach, not a top-down one. The coach is there to support, guide, encourage, and empower employees, not provide them with solutions.

By asking open-ended questions on a regular basis, the coach puts the responsibility for finding solutions on the employee. The questions continue when it is time to evaluate the solutions the employee wanted to try. Together, employee and coach discuss what worked and what did not.

Trust

Create trust with employees and trust the process. <u>Do not provide coaching once and forget it</u>. Like many topics we have covered in this book, employees crave consistency and enjoy the stability of a strong leader. Like many relationships, you can pat someone on the back 1,000 times and they only remember the kick in the ass. Remember that before you hand out an ass-kicking. It might be better to pause and ask a few questions so you can keep that trust in place.

Be an active listener when you work with a teammate and make sure that you model the behavior you expect from your team. Establishing trust <u>takes time,</u> but it can be lost quickly with inconsistent behavior and lack of follow through.

TIPS FOR USING COACHING QUESTIONS

<u>Use mainly open-ended questions</u> (cannot be answered with "yes" or "no"). This type of question cannot be easily answered. There is no "right" or "wrong" answer. Open-ended questions cause an employee to really think about the answer and new possibilities.

Here are a few ideas:

- How would you improve your methods the next time you complete a task?
- How can I help you reach your goals?
- What are you struggling with at work?
- What are the areas of improvement that you wish to see addressed in our office?
- In what ways could I improve the coaching experience for you?

<u>Keep questions broad and expansive</u> (not "problem-solving"). Ask general questions. The more specific the question is, the more it may appear you are leading the employee toward a particular outcome.

For example: "What do you hope to accomplish with this presentation?" and then if the response is "Demonstrate that our product is the best choice for the client," respond with "What might you change in the presentation to better reach your goal?" This is instead of a narrower question like, "What slides could you delete to make the presentation more effective?" When employ-

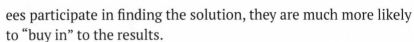

ees participate in finding the solution, they are much more likely to "buy in" to the results.

In general, ***avoid questions that start with "why."*** Questions that begin with "why" can often sound accusatory and make an employee feel defensive.

For example: "Tell me about your thought process" instead of "Why did/didn't you do [something?]" The first sentence assumes positive intent and comes across as curious and non-judgmental. The employee is more likely to feel comfortable expressing what happened than with the second sentence, which can imply that the decision they made was not correct and put them on the defensive.

Keep the mindset that <u>the employee has the solution</u>, and the manager's role is to facilitate their finding the wisdom within. Resist the urge to tell the employee how to do something. Allow the employee to think through things on their own. Always ask before you advise. Allowing the employee to come to their own solution will facilitate their development; allow them to learn more than if you tell them what to do; create an employee "buy in" to the solution; and allow you to remain open to other ways of doing things.

Assume positive intent. Appear curious, not critical. Even in the face of what appears to be a negative situation, allow yourself to remain open to other perspectives. You may learn there was a perfectly logical reason for the employee to do what they did. It may be that when something first appears negative on the surface, it has a more neutral or positive outcome. If the situation did not work out well, but there was a logical and positive reason behind it, focus on the learning in the situation.

Listen more than you talk. Give the employee the opportunity to really feel "heard." This is a strategy that builds trust with employees. You are also allowing the employee to find the solution instead of giving it to them.

Do not say what you would have done differently. A coaching mindset recognizes that there are many ways to get the job done and many different work styles that can all be effective. Your goal is not to create another version of you. Focusing too much on your own personal work style can be limiting.

Do not interrupt, be distracted or focus on what you will say next. Being fully present with the employee will show that you care about them, which will help establish trust.

What are examples of questions you can ask when coaching an employee?

First, my favorite way to phrase things is to start the question with "Tell me about ..." This is an easy way to make sure you are not asking close-ended questions. "Tell me about your approach to the project" or "Tell me about what happened with the client." These are always good lead-in questions to understand where the employee is coming from before you ask second and third level questions to draw out details.

1. What is the best next step (instead of what type of meeting do you need to have to move the project forward?)

2. What other approaches might you take next time? *vs.* Why did you think that was a good idea?

3. What can you learn from this? *vs.* Well, you won't do that again, will you?

4. To ensure we are on the same page, please tell me your understanding of the assignment *vs.* That is clear, isn't it?

5. What could you have changed about ... (situation)?

6. Can you tell me what led you to take that approach with ... (the other team member, patient, etc)?

7. What will it take to make you successful in this role or project?

8. Tell me more about that. (When the person hasn't provided details, or you don't thoroughly understand the situation.)

9. Help me to understand … (Puts the responsibility on the manager for not having understood.)

10. Tell me more about why you feel this way. (You can reflect, "You said you don't think that you are as challenged as you would like to be. Tell me more about why you feel this way.")

11. What's holding you back?

12. What is happening right now around [this issue]?

13. What have you done so far?

14. What effect did it have?

15. What is your goal/desired outcome in this situation?

16. What do you propose?

17. What is your plan?

18. What are some different ways that you might approach this situation?

19. What are some ways that you could make [stated desired result] happen?

20. What could be your next step?

21. What options do you have?

22. What would happen if you did nothing? (Helps solve the problem by "not solving" it.)

How do you assess the impact of coaching?

There are several ways to assess the impact. This can be done through performance metrics, employee surveys, and conversations. You must be willing to find your starting point to assess the impact. This is done in the same way (metrics, employee surveys, and conversations). When we are coaching teammates, we are creating trust, accelerating development, and increasing their engagement.

Key Points to Remember

1. Avoid disempowering statements. Ask questions to help your employees find their own answers.
2. Have a *growth* mindset over a *fixed* mindset. Do not think someone can't do something just because they didn't do it right once before.
3. Coaching encourages creativity and productivity, which leads to employees being committed and invested in the workplace and their supervisor.

COMPENSATION

Raise your hand if you have ever thought you would be willing to take a pay cut to be happier in your job. You are not alone. Money is not the biggest motivator for more than a third of the workforce. 36 percent of employees surveyed by PWC[10] would give up $5,000 a year in pay if it meant being happier and more engaged in their work.

Every CEO of a "Best Place to Work" that I have talked to agreed that while they have to be competitive in the wage scale, they are not trying to be the highest paying organization in their field. They want to highlight all the other areas we are talking about to attract top talent to their company. This is more important than ever at the time of this writing as the labor market for skilled workers is the tightest it has ever been, and much of what is covered above is becoming the "baseline" for top performing companies. *You must do the things in this book in order to compete.*

We are not going to go deep into the compensation rabbit-hole. I strongly believe, and the data suggests that you should have a competitive wage along with some form of incentive plan for everyone on your team. This is going to vary greatly by industry and role but I do think it is worth touching on some of the high

---

[10] *https://www.pwc.com/gx/en/services/people-organisation/publications/workforce-of-the-future.html*

points of compensation since it does become part of your culture (whether you like it or not).

HOW DO THE BEST COMPENSATE?

Here are a few of the unique ways the best in class compensates beyond salary:

- **Career planning and development**—Not only do they help people to plan, but they also provide resources and compensation for gaining knowledge. We talked a great deal about how the education and performance management process play a role in creating a great culture. Not only do these processes keep people engaged, but they are also viewed as part of the compensation package (if you position them as such).

- **Pay overtime to exempt employees**—We had Tom Pietras from Bauknight Pietras & Stormer, PA speak at an event we hosted a few years back about the topic of creating an awesome workplace. This compensation policy was one that several people talked about stealing after the event. Tom made mention of how his firm pays salaried exempt employee's overtime. They also have a comp time policy where their exempt (non-exempt employees are ineligible for comp time in most cases as it is a violation of the Fair Labor Standards Act which aims to protect worker's rights) can also take this as time off. Imagine, being a salaried exempt employee and being paid overtime when you work over 40 hours! This sounds too good to be true.

- **Rich PTO policy with flexibility**—Providing people with time away and making sure they take it is important to retaining talent. We are seeing people get more creative and bring their PTO policy into this century. You should really benchmark your PTO policy against not just your industry but companies that are hiring the people you want to hire.

We had a client who was benchmarking their PTO policy against others in their industry who do not give a lot of PTO to their hourly staff, but she was trying to hire a key administrative staff member and give her the same policy. You need to get creative and offer what is fair and equitable for the role. Remember, you are going to pay the salary, either way—this is not additional pay. If you can make someone happier, more productive, and more engaged with one extra week of vacation, this is a no-brainer.

- **Onsite fitness facility or gym memberships**—This keeps your team happy and healthy so they can be a complete person. As your team grows, I love doing events like "Biggest Loser" or the steps challenges to build positive momentum around healthy behaviors. We have a client who has a personal trainer come to the office every Tuesday and Thursday to do a "Boot Camp" in their parking lot for anyone interested. If you are a small business, look at doing things like this with neighboring businesses, or just give out gym memberships. We provide our staff with gym memberships at the gym across the street and encourage them to step out and exercise during the workday.

- **Free stocked fridge and snacks**—This is such a great "perk" for so many people. It can save people time and money, it creates some "collision" where the snacks because people can connect there, and you can provide healthy items for your team. I have seen how impactful this can be firsthand. We always have plenty of snacks, coffee, and water on hand for our team. I do not believe they should have to pay for all that while they are here in the building. The more extreme example is SAS in Cary, NC which has a five-star spa, Starbucks, childcare, and fine dining all on their campus, which employees can take advantage of. The least I can do is buy some protein bars!

- **Beer in the fridge**—You know your team. *Can they handle a fridge full of beer?* If so, by all means. We have had to implement some rules around this but always have something on hand for when the occasion calls for it. Make sure that you have rules in place (drinking and driving, no drinking by minors, is it locked up, etc.) if you're going to have alcohol on site. Check all legalities and liabilities that might be associated with this in your state.

- **Incentives**—There are plenty of examples of "one-off" incentives you can do for your team. You can send the team home after a half-day for goals hit, provide team bonuses, prizes for contests, and much more. Look back at the Chapter 9 on Employee Recognition for ideas on things you can do to keep your team engaged in a project or incentivized to hit a deadline. Incentives can keep morale high.

WHERE DOES COMPENSATION FIT IN THE PERFORMANCE MANAGEMENT PROCESS?

People have long held on to the thought process that an annual performance review equates to an employee getting a raise. This really failed us after the last recession when many employers stopped giving raises and then stopped giving performance reviews. **You should really pull the two apart from each other.** While this does not mean that performance will not impact your ability to get a raise, it does mean that you should not sit down in the annual performance review meeting and then say, "ok, great, all of that means you get a 3 percent raise."

There are a lot of reasons this is a bad idea, but it starts with the fact that you might not be able to give raises every year, so you want to be able to communicate that effectively—and not have to argue over the merits of the raise based on the feedback that should be able to be given freely in a performance conversation.

COMPENSATION EQUALITY

When it comes to compensation, you should be fair regardless of the person's gender, sexuality, hair color, or any other crazy thing you are biased against. Just because someone made $32,000 per year doing the job somewhere else and you would normally pay $45,000, does not mean you should try to get them for less. We all understand budgets at smaller companies, but don't short-change someone because their last employer did. Pay someone a fair wage to do the job. Pay them based on their value to the company.

HOW TO MANAGE A MULTI-GENERATIONAL TEAM

Finish this sentence: Millennials are tech_____.

Savvy?... *wrong* ... that is a common myth.

Millennials are not tech *savvy*; they are tech dependent. They have no idea how a phone was made or how it works—they just know that they cannot live without it. As a matter of fact, *who* made most of these gadgets that they can't live without? Baby Boomers like Steve Jobs, Bill Gates, and Jeff Bezos.

When a millennial wakes up in the morning, they post on Snapchat. They spend all day communicating via different forms of electronic messaging applications. The millennial generation's entire world is digital—according to a study by PWC, 41 percent of Millennials said they would rather communicate electronically than face-to-face or over the telephone.

Tech savvy ... not so much. *Tech dependent*? Ding. Ding. Ding.

That is just one of the myths surrounding the millennial generation (*credit to Jason Dorsey on that observation*).

WHAT MAKES MILLENNIALS SO IMPORTANT?

Millennials are the most important generation in the workforce. If you are a Boomer or Gen X'er and you disagree, it is because you think this generation cannot get ahead without the training and expertise that you have. This is true. However, you are a fool if you don't see the value in sharing that information with them. It is *the only way* to bring your organization to the next level. That is why, even though this section is titled "How to manage a multi-generational team" we are going to focus on millennials. We get 1000 percent more questions/comments, and concerns about this than any other topic related to the multi-generational team (Is that because the other generations complain more???? I kid. I kid. Don't get your undies in a bunch, boomers.) I am a Gen X'er and we like to play peacekeeper between the Boomers and the Millennials. I am not sure if this section is going to help my cause.

Millennials are your consumers.

In 2017, Millennials surpassed Boomers for spending in the market and they are already going to spend $1.3 trillion this year. So, even if you have no Millennials in your workforce, it is a good practice to understand your customer as they will continue to be a growing segment of your consumer base.

MILLENNIALS ARE SMART.

They are the best-educated generation in history[11]. 61 percent of Millennials have attended college, which is 15 percent more than Boomers. This is because Boomers have done a great job of letting their children know the importance and value of a good education in the marketplace.

---

[11]   *http://www.leadscon.com/18-statistics-that-marketers-need-to-know-about-millennials/*

MILLENNIALS ARE YOUR TEAM.

Finally, *Millennials make up half of the workforce.* You cannot ignore half of the workforce, and you cannot ignore the challenges that come with it.

WHO ARE THE MILLENNIALS? WHAT DO THEY CARE ABOUT?

Millennials are behind. Today's 28-year-olds are 3-5 years behind prior generations. They graduated later, they are getting married later (if at all) and they are starting their careers and having kids later. They are experiencing delayed adulthood.

Ironically, I often see the hypocrisy of parents who would tell their kids to take their time and travel overseas after graduation, only to have it negatively influence hiring decisions later.

CHARACTERISTICS OF MILLENNIALS:

- **Socially Conscious**—The average Millennial saw their parents sacrifice their lives for jobs with big companies that were scandal-ridden, only to have their company turn around and lay them off when times were tough. Millennials want to be a part of an organization that is cause-driven.

- **Team players**—Millennials have been playing sports since they were young. They are used to working in teams and performing as a unit.

- **Continuous learners/highly educated**—The best-educated generation in history. Millennials are smart. Education is highly valued.

- **Digital Native**—Gen Y has never had to adapt to technology, it has always been a part of their life. My mother-in-law (*who is amazing, I love you, Miss Annette!*) tells me a story about how my little brother-in-law could not figure out how to open the car door when the battery went in the remote key. He just figured that there was no way in if that key fob did not unlock the car electronically.

- **Optimistic**—It is strange how optimistic this generation is, considering the immense student loan debt they carry when leaving school, and the turmoil in the world. The average millennial has $27,000 in student loan debt when they graduate, but you always hear the same mantra, "It will all work out."

The Millennials create a unique breed of employee that the workforce has never seen before. Someone who cares about *why* they get up and go to work. Someone who wants to make a *real* impact. Someone who wants to know what their future holds with the company. *Do not be scared.* These are all good things.

Many employers are choosing to resist the characteristics that make the Millennial generation so special and simply try to make them adapt to the "old way" of doing things. While there is certainly merit in experience and proven processes, you have to be willing to adapt.

GENERATIONAL TENSION

I was talking to a group a couple of months ago about "Millennials in the Workforce" when the room grew a little tense. In the back of the room, a Millennial chimed up after hearing a comment from a Boomer in the front of the room,

"You all just don't understand how things work nowadays."

The Boomer responded back,

"You want everything handed to you. Work is not supposed to be fun."

It was **on**.

The friction between Boomers and Millennials is natural. After all, the Millennials are the children of … you guessed it, Boomers! How could you create better tension than putting parents in the workplace with people who act exactly like their kids and vice versa?

We are going to cover some of the challenges created by multiple generations in the workforce and how you can turn these challenges into strengths for your company. The focus on a lot of this section will be around understanding what different generations want from work and how you can make your company a place where all generations can thrive.

Challenge #1: Generational Tension

A few months back, I was coaching a new manager from a local company on how to deal with a problem employee. She told me that the person spoke to her like she did not know what she was talking about and didn't listen to any of the things she had to say.

"Why do you think that is?" I asked.

"It is because I am young enough to be his daughter and he doesn't respect me," she said.

All that this employee wanted was to be <u>empowered</u> to do their job, and all this manager wanted was to be <u>respected</u> as a peer. They didn't understand that once they both provided each other with that small victory, they could move mountains **together**.

Sometimes the gap is so small, we miss the point completely.

Fight Tension with Growth Opportunities

One of the best ways to eliminate the tension between generations is to put them in a collaborative environment where they can help each other. We all have strengths, and nothing feels better than doing something you are good at. Here are a few ways you can put people in a position to succeed with each other:

- **Collaboration**—Set up multi-generational work teams and create "win-win" situations for your team.

- **Cross training**—By training team members in multiple roles and disciplines, you not only create a wealth of knowledge within your company, but you can also create a better understanding and appreciation for fellow team members by seeing the struggles of others' roles in the organization.

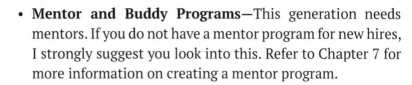

- **Mentor and Buddy Programs**—This generation needs mentors. If you do not have a mentor program for new hires, I strongly suggest you look into this. Refer to Chapter 7 for more information on creating a mentor program.

Challenge #2: Turnover

Can you guess the average tenure of Millennial employees? Two years. In comparison, the average tenure for Gen X employees is five years and seven years for Baby Boomers.

One of the primary reasons Millennials are more likely to change jobs is because they are not willing to stick around if they do not believe they are receiving any personal benefit or growth. They listened to their parents stay in jobs that they didn't like only to get laid off when things weren't going well or to hang for years and years unhappily.

While they have grown up in a much more structured environment, the educational system has been altered to teach autonomy. Choose your workstation, choose your group, this is what they have become accustomed to. You can't ignore this when creating the workplace of tomorrow.

Reduce Turnover with Flexibility

Millennials want flexibility with assignments. This is one of the most important attributes in a desirable workplace. Here are a few easy things you can do to provide flexibility:

- **Core hours**—Create "core hours" that people are expected to be at the office, but they can be flexible on the other hours they work. For example: core hours are 10 a.m.- 4 p.m., some people will come in at 8 a.m. and work until 4 p.m., others will come in at 10 a.m. and work until 4 p.m. and then work again at 8 p.m. that evening. You should be focused on the results, not the hours.
- **Variable workstations**—This can take on a variety of forms whether it be encouraging people to work in the conference spaces, work from home, work from a close client or part-

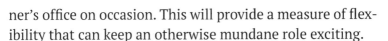

ner's office on occasion. This will provide a measure of flexibility that can keep an otherwise mundane role exciting.

- **Don't micromanage**—Do your best to not hover over a Millennial. Set goals and desired results and show them what those results look like. This will provide some flexibility and maybe even creativity in completing the task at hand.

- **Social recognition**—Meet them where they live. How nice would it be for an employee to retweet a company message that was highlighting what a great job they did? Don't you think they would share that with friends and family, therefore solidifying your place in the market as well?

Challenge #3: Succession Planning

Retirement, especially as it pertains to the Baby Boomer generation bears a great impact on the current workforce and the future of your organization. With the youngest Baby Boomers turning 52 this year, you must incorporate effective succession planning into your strategic operations. By developing your team and creating the type of place people want to work, you will make your succession plan simpler.

Understanding that Millennials will make up 50 percent of the workforce in the coming years, don't you think they should be involved in the leadership strategy? Many organizations continue to look at tenure and experience as the only barometer when identifying high potential future leaders. This is a huge mistake that could result in massive turnover if you are not careful.

The great news is this: Millennials have now been in the workforce long enough to have tenure, experience, and most importantly the ability to lead their peers. Now you need to groom them for the roles you need them to take on in the future. Take the steps outlined below, combined with the actions above to prepare yourself for the leadership team of the future.

- **Step 1:** *Future needs*—Consider the organization's future leadership needs to Identify the short-term and long-term vision and direction of the organization. Analyze future leadership requirements for products and services offered now and in the future.

- **Step 2:** *The right fit*—Identify the competencies and experiences necessary for success in future leadership roles. Perform an analysis of the leadership positions to define the qualifications that a successful job incumbent would possess.

- **Step 3:** *Assess current talent*—Find the obvious and hidden talent within your current organization.

- **Step 4:** *Develop pathways*—Create a roadway of how an identified high potential employee would attain the qualifications defined in Step 2. Create an individual development plan for your future leaders to follow.

- **Step 5:** *Measure progress*—Follow up with the employee as to how they are doing in achieving the desired qualifications for a future leadership position. Also, continually evaluate the organization's evolving leadership needs, and periodically repeat Steps 1-4.

You did it! You finished this section of the book. You get a participation trophy!

Unfortunately, there are no participation trophies in business. You cannot ignore half of the workforce that also represents the majority of the marketplace and expect to be successful. You must adapt to succeed. I know that each of you will do what it takes to make your workplace successful for all generations.

As leaders of our companies, we have to equip our existing team for situational leadership and an understanding of the other generation they are working with. The importance of harnessing the energy and talent of the largest percentage of our workforce cannot be overstated.

CHAPTER 10 TAKEAWAYS

After reading this chapter, my hope is that you have a better understanding on everything from coaching and compensation, to leading a multi-generational workplace. Let's reflect on some of the key points from Chapter 10.

- Don't be an a**hole when it comes to leading your team. Show empathy toward your employees.

- Provide your team with regular feedback as this will help them improve their performance on the job and in future positions.

- Your role as a coach can define someone's career. Give your team the support they need to be good at what they do.

- To prevent tension in a multi-generational workplace, create a collaborative environment that gets employees working toward the same goal.

CONCLUSION

Well, you have made it to the end of *Ping-Pong Is Not A Strategy*. We covered a number of topics in this book, and I want to make sure you walk away with actionable directives to start making changes at your organization today.

As I mentioned at the beginning of the book, it is not necessary to implement every strategy. First, you have to determine what your company is lacking the most and begin there. Do not rush into making any changes, especially those that will affect your team and organization. Your employees are your most important asset, and you should treat them as so.

If you can recall, I posed three questions to you at the start of the book. Can you now answer "yes" to all three?

1. Do you believe your employees are your company's most important asset?

2. Are you committed to building the type of place people want to work?

3. Are you willing to step outside your comfort zone to make that happen?

If you are still able to answer those questions without hesitation, today is the day to get started. Still not convinced? Consider going back and rereading the chapters that would be most beneficial to your organization. Being intentional and consistent are the two most important components to remember when making any changes to your workplace culture. Your mindset matters. Your ideas matter. This matters.

I have compiled the below summary of the most important takeaways from the book. If you have yet to scribble any notes within these pages, I recommend doing it in this section.

MAJOR TAKEAWAYS

- The mindset of an entire leadership team can negatively impact how well a "good" hire does their job.

- If you do not take action about where your workplace is headed, it will eventually end up way off course.

- Leadership is the secret to success. Your company's culture is only as good as your leadership.

- You can't rely on someone else to create the culture you envision. It begins with you.

- Not being thorough in your screening process can cost you thousands and destroy your culture.

- Hire slow and fire fast.

- You only have one chance to make a first impression.

- Employee onboarding is proven to have the biggest impact on retention and engagement.

- Showing appreciation for your teammates is more than just a one-time thing. Consistency is key.

- Provide your team with regular feedback as this will help them improve their performance on the job and in future positions.

- Your role as a coach can define someone's career. Give your team the support they need to be good at what they do.

Typically, this would be the part in the book where I tell you that you are ready to spread your wings and fly—or something like that. But you can't be expected to fly if you don't know where you are going. Look at the

MAJOR TAKEAWAYS

checklist of directives below, which will provide you with a map of where to get started with implementing the strategies within this book.

❑ Define your Core Values. Complete Core Values exercise with team.

❑ Review your leadership team. Do their mindsets align with your Core Values?

❑ Audit your hiring process. Make changes to engage and retain "A" players.

❑ Create employee personas for ideal candidates.

❑ Develop an employee onboarding process that assimilates new hires into your culture.

❑ Assign mentors to each member of your team, including new hires and tenured employees.

❑ Develop training programs for each type of learner—visual, audio, kinesthetic.

❑ Put training on everyone's calendar.

❑ Start completing performance reviews on a routine basis.

❑ Recognize the actions of your team by creating a system for appreciation.

❑ Create your own R.E.A.C.T. model for coaching employees.

❑ Determine how you want to compensate employees beyond their salary.

Ready to make a positive change to your organization's culture? Start NOW.

BIBLIOGRAPHY

Preface

http://www.nytimes.com/1998/10/13/science/placebos-prove-so-powerful-even-experts-are-surprised-new-studies-explore-brain.html

Chapter 1

https://news.gallup.com/poll/241649/employee-engagement-rise.aspx

https://www.dalecarnegie.com/en/resources/emotional-drivers-of-employee-engagement

Chapter 3

https://resources.globoforce.com/research-reports/findings-from-the-shrm-globoforce-employee-recognition-survey-employee-experience-as-a-business-driver

Chapter 5

https://online.alvernia.edu/articles/cost-employee-turnover/

Chapter 7

https://www.pwc.com/gx/en/industries/financial-services/publications/millennials-at-work-reshaping-the-workplace-in-financial-services.html

https://community.mis.temple.edu/mis0855002fall2015/files/2015/10/S.M.A.R.T-Way-Management-Review.pdf

Chapter 9

http://go.globoforce.com/rs/862-JIQ-698/images/
SHRM2017_GloboforceEmployeeRecognitionReportFi-
nal.pdf?_ga=2.163866175.1806273419.1562496873-
1788112948.1562496873

Chapter 10

http://www.leadscon.com/18-statistics-that-marketers-need-to-
know-about-millennials/

https://www.pwc.com/gx/en/services/people-organisation/publica-
tions/workforce-of-the-future.html

https://jasondorsey.com/

Made in the USA
Middletown, DE
15 October 2023

40534076R00113